THE INTERIM

THE INTERIM DIRECTOR

40 PROJECTS IN THE WILDERNESS
. . . and a lot of sound advice

Alasdair Drysdale

Management Books 2000

First published in 2015 by Management Books 2000 Ltd
36 Western Road
Oxford OX1 4LG
Tel: 0044 (0) 1865 600738
Email: info@mb2000.com
Web: www.mb2000.com

British Library Cataloguing in Publication Data is available

ISBN 9781852527464

*It is not the strongest of the species that survives,
nor the most intelligent that survives.
It is the one that is most adaptable to change.*

Charles Darwin

CONTENTS

PREFACE

Los Angeles International Airport, 3am

I've just flown in from Cleveland, Ohio, where the snow is so bad that they've invented a special category 4 severity because the usual categories 1, 2 and 3 will not suffice. Even at this time of night LA is decidedly warm, and I'm ridiculously and uncomfortably over-dressed. There are dozens of cars around and hundreds of people, but no taxis, and the situation does not look promising.

Suddenly an enormous white stretch-limo with darkened windows pulls in effortlessly from the chaos and halts in front of me. One window slides down. The driver, an immaculately dressed gent who looks like a much larger version of Barry White, purrs "You goin' someplace?"

"Placentia," I reply, shedding some of my Nanook-of-the-North garments.

We agree 40 bucks and I slide into the back.

"You like music?" asks the big guy. "I'm a piano man."

I think that means that I ought to be a piano man, too.

"George Shearing? Oscar Peterson?" I suggest, trying to sound casual, as if I would actually know either of them from Ramsey Lewis, or for that matter, Jerry Lee Lewis.

"Man, you talkin' my language," he murmurs, and the big limo pulls effortlessly out of LAX on to the I-105, heading for Placentia to the sound of rippling ivories.

I'm half listening to the music, half trying to recognise points on the route, to work out whether we really are going to Placentia or whether I've ended up in some movie or other by mistake. But he takes me straight to my motel, and I give him an extra 10 bucks for such a smooth journey.

He probably owns a luxury pad up in Canyonlands by now.

FOREWORD
by Ad van der Rest, MIIM
Chairman of The Institute of Interim Management (IIM)*

Many business people would be deeply fearful of the roaming lifestyle undertaken by Alasdair Drysdale, moving from interim assignment to interim assignment without a safety net, because job security is still valued in work even if it is increasingly an illusion.

Alasdair's exploration of 40 projects as an interim director is a delight because it gives a real insight into what interim directors, managers and executives actually do to resolve the deep-seated challenges they find, assuming that the incumbent executives don't further add to the obstacles. With disarming honesty and pragmatism, he litters his tome with nuggets of advice on what works and occasionally doesn't work, in practice.

Not all interim directors have quite as colourful an international career as Alasdair, but there is much here that would benefit those considering taking a leap of faith by establishing a professional interim business of their own, or otherwise if only to underline that this lifestyle reminiscent of "Mission: Impossible" and the cavalry galloping over the hill in the nick of time, is not for them.

Even for people who have no intention of 'going interim' there are many techniques here to super-change permanent employment, because a focus on results, simplicity and boldness often work really well in permanent roles, too.

The Institute of Interim Management (IIM) is the UK's professional body for independent professionals operating at board or near-board level as interim directors, managers and executives, in business on their own account. It welcomes such professionals to its ranks and offers free advice to those considering working for themselves in this way. You can contact the Institute of Interim Management at iim.org.uk or by telephone on +44 (0)800 030 4716.

IN THE BEGINNING

According to the records (I have no personal memory of the event) I was born in Perth, UK in 1947, and later taken out by my mother to East Africa on a troopship to join my father, who had obtained work in Uganda. We lived in Jinja, Nairobi, Dar-es-Salaam and Mombasa, and while based at Mombasa I attended a rough-and-ready yet highly-regarded boarding school on the edge of Kikuyu land beyond Nairobi, a mile above sea-level.

Not fancying university and not having the faintest clue as to what I wanted to do, I did a 5-year apprenticeship with an uninspiring small Edinburgh firm, now no longer existent, to become a chartered accountant. Still not knowing what I wanted to do, I joined a firm with a much wider variety of financial work and spent several happy years with them.

Having become an experienced scuba diver in my spare time, I left the accountants to work full-time as a diver, starting in the North Sea, and then on to Nigeria, the South China Sea and the Arabian Gulf, where I became the superintendent of all of the company's diving operations in the region. We made solid profits and had no major accidents, but a lot of fun, thanks to a shrewd and very forward-thinking managing director, and a good crew.

After 7 years of sunning myself on the heli-decks of the world, I went back to the large accounting firm to handle receiverships, start-ups and various other non-recurring projects. This led to an offer to be the financial director of a company for whom I had raised a considerable amount of public-sector money. I accepted, but the managing director decided that I argued too much and fired me with a generous compensation after only a few weeks.

I made some phone calls, and two days later a contact in the recruitment business called and said "I've got just the job for you; a project with a manufacturing group."

I wasn't about to refuse.

DEFINITIONS

There have been endless discussions on various professional and social media sites as to the difference between an interim director and a consultant, so I may as well have my tuppence-worth on the subject.

Definition by style:
- A consultant says "This represents a significant window of opportunity."
- An interim director says "This is a good chance."

Definition by performance:
- A consultant is a Spitfire – sleek, delicate, high-altitude, high-profile (22,500 were built).
- An interim director is a Hurricane – rock-solid, tight-turning, go-anywhere and highly versatile (14,500 Hurricanes were built, and the 11,500 which were not sent to the Soviet Union accounted for 55% of all British and Commonwealth aerial victories from 1939 to 1945, a truly remarkable statistic).

The highest-scoring RAF ace in the Battle of Britain was a South African Hurricane pilot, and the highest-scoring RAF and Commonwealth ace in the entire 1939-45 war was... another South African Hurricane pilot. But the Spitfire received most of the glory, and still does.

Choice:
Whether clients want an Interim Director/ Hurricane or a Consultant/ Spitfire will therefore depend mainly upon their needs. There are many instances in which one can do the job of the other, and many other times when the client has to make a specific selection. There are also times when the two types have to work together, occasionally

with an initial degree of mutual suspicion, but for the most part happily and effectively.

Whether you are an interim director or a consultant, or even an innocent bystander, reading this book will do you no harm.

By the way: the names in this book are fictitious... but the people are real.

PART 1

THE EARLY DAYS:
BASIC PROJECTS

1. THE WINDOW GROUP

When a recruiter says "I've got just the job for you" it sometimes means that it's something you shouldn't touch, even with the proverbial barge-pole, but this particular recruiter has a greater knack of suiting candidates to posts than most of his competitors. The client is a group of window companies housed in two locations, the main one in the Scottish Borders and the other just off the M8, which is oddly referred to as "Central Scotland", despite being nowhere near the centre of Scotland (the English call the M62 "The North" with the same disregard for geographical accuracy).

The interview with the managing director is for two very different requirements:

- taking control of the finance function and producing some meaningful financial forecasts and reports
- doing some detailed costings of the products, for which there are almost no data

I tell him that I'm possibly the best in the business at producing well-structured and reliable forecasts, and probably the worst in the business at product costing. He replies that the costing requirement is secondary, and asks me to start immediately at the M8 factory near Edinburgh. Until now he has been running blind and is inevitably seriously concerned. He needs reliable forward-looking numbers. Fast.

The M8 factory is the smaller of the group's two UK locations, and contains only a windows production line, plus the finance department for both sites. The site in the Borders comprises all of the other offices, together with four operations:

- a manufacturing company that makes and fits PVC-U windows to order (as on the M8)

- a kit company that cuts and fits aluminium windows and doors on customer sites (the aluminium frames can be coated in various finishes)
- a systems company which sells a comprehensive range of components for customer companies throughout the UK to manufacture into specific windows and doors and fit the products into their customers' buildings
- a Dublin company that has been producing a separate range of windows for the Irish market (this range to be superseded by the UK range, which meets the Irish parameters)

The group has recently been acquired by a larger windows group headquartered in the south-east of England, and the larger group has clearly not done its due diligence investigation very diligently. To their credit, however, they have since hired two very experienced and hard-hitting directors: the managing director of the Scottish companies and an overall group financial director based in the south of England. For brevity I'll call them MD and FD. They are both incessantly demanding and stimulating to work for, and quick to recognise achievements, and much of what I've done since in my working life has stemmed from their well-directed guidance.

The first requirement is to produce a set of profit-and-cash forecasts that bear some relation to the real performance and capability of the group. Rule No 1 for the interim director is to score a quick goal, to give the client confidence, so I go hell-for-leather at building realistic forecast models. Before long there are 5 individual forecasts, intra-group eliminations and a total group forecast clattering away on the A4 spoke-wheel printer.

These go by fax (remember those machines?) to the MD, who is visiting Dublin, and the FD at HQ in south-east England. The response is immediate: why are my forecasts so far below the individual forecasts of the operating managers? My answer is "Because I haven't seen any figures that cause me to believe those forecasts" and I wait for the explosion.

It doesn't come; both of the recipients are hardened realists. Good.

Both the MD and the FD conclude rightly that if that's all the profit that can be expected, we must amend the organisation accordingly. That in turn leads to my doing a number of different models of the group in six possible formats, the outcome of which means that we shall have to close the factories in Edinburgh and Dublin and run the whole operation from the Scottish Borders factory, reducing the Dublin office to a sales outlet. On paper it is not the most profitable solution, but managerially it will be much more viable with all of the main operations under one roof; a sharp lesson that sometimes facts and structures are as important as the figures.

Much secretive planning follows before the bomb is dropped. The Dublin and Central Scotland employees take the news remarkably well for the most part, which is a great help (I don't think it is any great surprise to them; employees are generally quick to sense when their company is struggling), and we can thus concentrate on the reorganisation. The finance department is clearly not going to relocate and I have been interviewing for replacements, with some very good luck. Despite careful packaging, the equipment and the records arrive in the Scottish Borders factory (from now "the factory") in considerable disarray off the back of a van at the end of the financial year. Sabotage?

I needn't bore the reader with the minutiae of setting up an entirely new finance department at an entirely new (for those involved) location under a nearly-new financial controller (me), but somehow the department gets itself into shape in a short space of time, under the command of a no-nonsense management accountant, a resourceful systems accountant and commendably practical clerical assistants. Plenty of late-nights follow to get everything into shape.

With all of the product coming out of a single factory we have much less traffic in figures, but also less understanding of the accuracy and relevance of the numbers themselves in the absence of previous operation in the new configuration. Figures are typically available after the middle of each month, which means that we're firing blind 50% of the time. We need to reform that radically, although it appears to be the norm for the rest of the group based in the south-east of England.

On the wall of the processing office of the finance department we put up a number of flip-chart sheets, one for each of the major accounting systems, and each sheet having a line down the middle. Members of the finance team enter on the left side of each sheet every reason why we cannot produce monthly financial statements within 2 days of each month-end. Team members are then to write their proposed solutions on the right-hand side of the line.

Bear in mind, reader, that all computers of this era are stand-alone, with a maximum size of 640Kb (two-thirds of a megabyte), all printers are spoke-wheel, and the internet does not exist. Bank statements and invoices come in by post, so we are at the mercy of our bankers and suppliers when it comes to obtaining rapid information on cash and purchases.

D-Day... the finance department assembles in a room at the back of the factory, strictly incommunicado, even to the directors (fortunately, the room has no telephone, and mobile phones are as yet almost non-existent, not to mention hugely clunky and expensive). The problem sheets are up on the walls, and coffee and food are on constant supply. Apart from toilet breaks, nobody is to leave the room until we have a solution to every recorded problem and are able to produce detailed monthly results within two working days of each month-end for:

- two manufacturing companies and one components company distributing from the Scottish Borders throughout the UK via our own fleet
- one company distributing weekly, strictly to order, from the Scottish Borders to Northern Ireland and the Republic of Ireland
- one all-Ireland sales and support office
- one holding company in the Scottish Borders performing and recharging all central functions (finance, admin, personnel, transport, customer support, research and development, safety, property, etc.)
- a set of consolidated results showing the individual companies in columnar form for comparison

The finance department has been considering possible solutions to the rapid-accounting barriers for some weeks, and the brainstorming session goes remarkably well, most of the solutions being surprisingly simple. For example:

- all payments are to be processed (but not necessarily sent out) on the third last working day of the month, so that the purchasing figures, adjusted of course for goods received not yet invoiced, are completed accurately by the month-end, with help from the stock controllers
- sales persons and other travellers are to have their expense claims in on the same (third last) day, together with an estimate of any further costs between then and the month-end

And so on; it certainly isn't rocket science, but who needs that when simplicity works so well? The answers fill up the right-hand side of each of the sheets on the walls. There is, however, one remaining problem, and it's a big one; we need accurate month-end stock figures. As it happens, there is a meeting of the company managers that afternoon, and I interrupt them to say "Guys, if you can give us a reliable stock figure on Day 1 of each new month, we can give you detailed and accurate results on day 3. Can you do that?" It's not an unreasonable request, as we work on a 4-4-5 week basis rather than a calendar month, so the stock count is always carried out on a Sunday, when there is rarely any production to disrupt it .

The "Yes" replies are unanimous and instant, and so enthusiastic that I wonder if we have over-committed ourselves. However, the finance team go to work preparing for the next month-end on the agreed basis and the product managers organise rigorous stock counts. Some of the factory floor personnel are concerned at the amount of time that the counts will take, resulting in more overtime cost, but the riposte from the managers, quite correctly, is that the more stock counts they do, the faster and more accurate they will become. In time, the monthly stock counts become welcome, as they identify various issues that would otherwise remain unresolved.

With each monthly accounting period ending on a Sunday, the stock figures are provided to the finance team on the Monday. The monthly managers' meetings take place on the Wednesday, when the major issues from the month are still very much in mind. The managers go offsite to a hired lounge in a nearby hotel for the whole day, with all of the discussion topics fresh in their minds. Late in the morning the accountant appears with the draft results for all the companies for the month, so that any explanations and adjustments are agreed there and then. After lunch the accountant returns to the finance team and processes any adjustments agreed at the meeting with the managers, then places the final results on the managers' desks for their return in the late afternoon.

In one move, the group and its companies have gone from a state of perpetual ignorance to a permanent grasp of current reality. From then onward they will be looking at the future, not at the past.

There remains, however, one final task. On the Thursday morning, the fourth day of the new month, the accountant faxes five detailed sets of company accounts for the month of May plus a consolidated set down to HQ, inundating HQ's fax machine in the process. I receive a furious call from the group FD, demanding to know why we're cluttering up their fax system when they already had our April statements two weeks previously. I suggest that he looks at the date on the documents churning out of the machine. His reaction is typical: "May? Bloody hell! I'm getting on the blower to the rest of the group – if you guys can do it in two days for six sets of figures, they can each do it for one." We are the only outfit which has a sub-group.

We have gone from being the group's whipping-guys to being the blue-eyed guys, and he begins sending other controllers up to us to see how we manage our accounting. In today's communications environment this is all very old-hat, but the important lesson is that simplicity usually beats complexity, and that still applies today. It probably always will.

There is, however, much more to be done. We set up monthly finance sessions for the sales force and technical/R&D team, getting them to work out simple financial case studies. In particular, we focus them on margin rather than on sales value. At first they cannot believe that if your unit sale price is £100 and your margin is £15, and you reduce your selling price by 3%, i.e. £3, you will have to increase your volume by 25% to achieve the same monetary margin, and some of your overheads will of course also increase.

Over several sessions we instil in them:

- that our income is NOT our sales value... the income is our net margin
- sales value merely indicates the level of PAIN one must incur to achieve the net margin

We also give them cash flow examples to calculate, and increasingly we throw in typical complications such as slow debt recovery and poor stock control. These examples highlight the necessity for the sales team to liaise closely with the production and inventory managers. We then introduce an element of monthly performance pay for each salesperson, calculated on days of debt below 60 and net margin percentage on sales in each of their areas. At last we are chasing the targets that really matter; the sales force is helping with the cash collection process.

Then we set the sales force to identifying problems in our customers' businesses, to ensure that our customers are also robust, rather than being potential bad debts. The windows industry has a deserved reputation for being a "cowboy" industry and if our customers are running badly-controlled businesses, then that will impact adversely on us, sooner or later.

Importantly, we relocate our sales force into the research and development/ technical department, so that any problems (and also any useful ideas) encountered in the field are fed straight back to the designers.

In one week, I dig out my scruffy old oilfield overalls and safety boots and go out on one of the delivery trucks on its three-day run round the north-east of England. Not only does that reveal all sorts of interesting factors regarding the delivery process, it provides me with an inside view of how our customers are operating their businesses. Crowded and badly-organised production areas, disorderly over-stocking and poor debt collection procedures are rife. Having trained our sales force in financial fundamentals, we now set them about improving their customers' slackly-controlled businesses, and we send out members of our technical team to help our customers improve their production efficiency in a whole range of respects (maintenance, scheduling, stock ordering, etc.).

The result of this campaign is remarkably quick; our customers forge ahead when their operations are trimmed to the optimum operating levels and their loyalty to us increases greatly. Some customers who have hitherto held excessive stock of components are converted from a monthly delivery schedule to a two-weekly schedule, which greatly improves their working capital level, and hence their ability to pay us promptly.

Eventually, we run the same financial dynamics training for our customers that we have run for our sales force. Smart customers are less likely to hit the list of bad debts. Our credit controller now has time to coach our customers' credit controllers, further improving our cash flow.

One day I discover that when our ageing fleet of leased distribution vehicles is being replaced, our marketing team has instructed that all three of our long-range curtainsiders should be painted navy-blue, all of them.

I go ballistic. The general public, not noting the registration numbers, will think we only have one vehicle! But if the tractor units were painted three strong colours and the trailers were painted three softer colours (still adorned with the company logo), we would have nine different colour combinations and would appear to be a much larger company.

Moreover, the trailers are curtain-siders, so they could be painted a different colour on each side, giving us 18 colour combinations, and the public would think we are a VERY large company. This is what our marketing advisers should have been telling me, not the other way around. Unfortunately the liveries have all been applied, and we have a boring navy-blue fleet. That still rankles, a couple of decades after it happened. Or didn't happen, rather.

At this point there is a storm down south in the holding company boardroom, and the other directors dismiss the group managing director from the board, under provisions in the holding company's articles of association. Our local managing director heads south to help the group financial director control the group and I'm left in charge of our sub-group. However, the issue in question is that a much larger group wishes to acquire our holding company and despite a spirited defence by our group board (minus the ejected group managing director) the larger group takes us over in a hostile bid.

Although we are now one sub-group structurally and legally, our new owners split us into two of their existing divisions, removing at a stroke all of the synergy, economy and profitability we have built as a small, tightly-controlled sub-group. We do have the last word, however, when at the annual conference of the new larger group (now with 96 operating subsidiaries) they show slides of the performance of the subsidiaries and a large gasp goes up across the conference when our flagship company is shown to have 103% return on capital. The audience are amazed... very satisfying.

I become the deputy financial controller of the acquiring group, but apart from a couple of small investigative projects I'm told to keep strictly away from the 90-plus subsidiaries. The group finance function is mainly accounting-driven and is kept well away from performance issues.

The nadir comes when I point out that the overheads-to-sales ratio that the group uses to compare the trends of its subsidiaries is entirely misleading. Some of the companies which return acceptable overheads-to-sales ratios show a very different picture when the overheads-to-net-margin ratios are calculated. One subsidiary I select at random is in a steadily-steepening decline and I publish its overheads-to-net-margin trend anonymously (multiplied by a constant to preserve the ratios without identifying the company), so that the other subsidiaries will check their own trends and take action. I receive a flea in my ear for my troubles, despite having demonstrated clearly that some of the businesses are on the slide without any action being taken.

Following further inertia I give the group 6 months' notice shortly after that, upon which I'm given the enjoyable project of completely rebuilding the group's disjointed and difficult-to-operate budgeting system. There are few easier jobs than that, so I have a pleasant last few months designing and building a push-button budgeting and consolidation system. After I have left the group I phone a few controllers to ensure that the budgeting system hasn't caused them any problems, but they confirm that it's watertight, simple to operate and demands realism in the input.

I'm now on the street, unemployed after an "interim" role which has lasted 3 years! I scratch around to no avail for a couple of months, then receive a call from the former manager of one of the companies in my first group.

Am I available? You bet I am. This time it really will be an interim job.

LESSONS

A. *Judging the level of stretch in a budget can be tricky. If your management team is not performing up to the level required, you may have to give them a tough budget to get them moving, but if you stretch the budget too far, they will regard it as unrealistic and admit defeat from the very beginning. This happens in groups who keep stretching their subsidiaries year after year.*

The right level of budget is one that can be achieved by your team working hard and intelligently, given even breaks (some good, some bad). Bad breaks can cause managers to give up chasing the budget, but on the other hand good breaks can cause them to slacken off, as they can achieve their budget targets without the level of effort originally envisaged.

In the case of the window group with a huge amount of lost ground to make up, the budget had to be tough, but the management team were judged on the effort and initiative they put into the process as much as on the results achieved. This kept them motivated, and eventually they began hitting and then exceeding their targets.

B. *CYA... if you are instructed to issue a forecast which in your opinion is unrealistically high and there is no further argument possible, obey the instruction and confirm your obedience in writing with an email stating that you have prepared/ amended the forecast "as instructed" and mention your reservations regarding the numbers. And don't forget to keep a copy!*

"CYA" is not an espionage agency; it stands for "cover your ass".

C. *Financial results are not always the only factor in decision-making. The first forecasts I prepared for the window group showed a better performance for the Central Scotland factory than for the Scottish Borders factory. However, the managing director considered (correctly, as it turned out emphatically) that the management and workforce in the Borders had a greater capability. It was a courageous and very astute call on his part.*

D. *The commonest error in business is concentrating on the sales figures. The real revenue of any business is the NET VARIABLE MARGIN.*

E. *I once found a business whose research and development department was located on the US Eastern seaboard and whose international sales office was in Western Europe. I asked the financial director how the boffins knew exactly what the markets wanted and he merely rolled his eyes. Built-in failure! In the window group our practice of housing the sales force in the technical/R&D department paid great dividends; the sales force fully understood the products and the designers fully understood the customer requirements.*

F. *Repetition can greatly improve performance. Our requirement for a monthly stock-count was initially very disruptive, with some strange results, but enforcing it as a monthly process meant that the stock team became slicker and faster to the point where we could rely fully on their numbers.*

2. HEAVY METAL EUROPE

I can't be very specific about this one, because there aren't very many businesses in this particular industry. Suffice it to say that they are involved in heavy manufacture, making an industrial product of which I've never heard before. They have factories and sales organisations throughout the world.

A former colleague, who has recently joined the group, explains that his company has acquired a subsidiary in mainland Europe, and he wants a million euros taken out of the company's cost structure.

You shouldn't take on jobs that you don't know how to do, but when there's nothing else on the horizon and you don't have much breadth of experience, it's hard to say "no". I take a day to plan to myself how to go about this project and then I agree to do it. After the briefest of briefings I'm on an aircraft to the Low Countries, wondering just what I've let myself in for.

The local Managing Director, an erudite man from a very different part of Europe, is very helpful in intent, but is not close enough to the detail of the operation to suggest any lines of enquiry, nor even any advantageous starting point. However, after more than a week of interviewing and searching I come to the conclusion from my own investigations that any fat there may have been in the business has already been taken out in previous exercises. Any further reduction in personnel or facilities will damage the business, perhaps seriously, at management level.

With some trepidation I call in on my colleague in UK, and tell him the bad news (or at least, the situation as I see it). To my surprise he readily accepts my view. "That doesn't really surprise me," he says, "but what I really needed was someone over there who thinks the way we do over here." He then tells me that there is nothing further for me to do in mainland Europe, but that there are various jobs to be done in UK and Europe in tightening up some of the procedures and coaching a couple of the managers. These unremarkable tasks take a few weeks, after which the client seems happy and I go cheerfully on my way.

A strange, fragmented assignment, but welcome nevertheless.

During the project a small event occurs which has no bearing on my work, but which shakes me to the core. Asleep in a hotel in a Belgian town, I'm woken by the sound of bagpipes playing a lament, and it sounds as if the piper is directly below my window. I struggle from my bed and lurch over to the window but can see nothing in the pitch-darkness. The noise, coming from another street, is almost deafening, bouncing off the stone walls and cobbled streets of the town. A glance at my watch tells me it is 0600 and then I note the date, bearing the number 11.

Still sleepy, I'm puzzled... why the pipes?

Then it dawns upon me.

It is the 11th of November 1993; three-quarters of a century after the end of the Great War. I'm not particularly emotional, but I stand there transfixed with tears streaming down my face as the blood-chilling lament from the pipes reverberates off the stone walls and cobbled streets of the little town in the pitch-darkness. Unlike me, the inhabitants will know from the instant they hear the lament what it commemorates.

LESSONS

A. *Given that I haven't achieved anything, it's hard to extract any lessons from this project. The UK head office of the group has struck me as a very practical and reasonable team, and therefore I can only conclude that some previous members of the management team have engendered poor relations with the European subsidiaries. Once such bad relations exist, it can take a long time to repair them.*

B. *The mantra "Reduce the staff numbers" is one of the first reactions when a business starts performing poorly. It may help, but only if the essential functions of those persons discontinued are effectively* *assumed by the remaining staff. Once staff numbers have been reduced below the level needed to make the business perform, the remaining staff increasingly develop a fatalistic attitude and care less and less about the effectiveness of their own individual actions and the status of the team as a whole. The usual result is that the business spirals rapidly downwards.*

3. MANAGEMENT TRAINING

My former sub-group which was taken over (see project no 1) has remained strong on training despite the lack of interest from its new owners, and has noted that many of its customer companies are somewhat haphazardly managed. They therefore ask me to run training courses for their customers on a regional basis.

The courses are simple and concentrate on two issues:

- producing rapid, reliable and relevant management information
- using that information to run and constantly improve the business

I use the same material as I have used for my original employers (on project no 1) as there is nothing in it needing updated. The only difference is that I encourage informal dialogue amongst our customers throughout the two-day session. Although they are each other's competitors they have a large number of problems and pet-hates to share, which makes for a very collaborative course. In addition to bringing home the essential financial dynamics and rules of good business, we raise many commercial problems for which a variety of possible solutions are aired.

Above all, we get companies actually *using* their numbers instead of just producing them and then leaving them in a file.

LESSONS

A. *The mathematical basics of good business apply to all businesses, especially in the case of manufacturing activities. I have subsequently used the same course for many other businesses without needing to alter much of the material.*

B. *Although businesses are in competition, it can be beneficial for them to discuss problems with each other for mutual advancement. If some businesses are perceived by their customers to perform badly, it can harm the reputation of that sector as a whole, a situation which was notoriously prevalent in the early days of the PVC-U windows industry.*

4. THE GRUMPY MD

The financial director who had galvanised our window group (see chapter 1) calls me to look at a manufacturing subsidiary of the group he has joined lately; in his opinion it is carrying far too much inventory. On arriving at the company I find that the local managing director disagrees with this view, stating that his level of inventory is right for the business and that there are no non-useful items anywhere. I reply that the project will therefore be a very short one. His response is best described as a grunt.

Actually, it is a short project... but not for the reason he has given. Trawling through his inventory print-outs discloses all manner of slow-moving items (fortunately, most of them usable eventually) and probing the darkest recesses of his factory reveals various partly-built products which clearly have been lying in that state for a long time and don't look like being sold.

The MD is patently not a figures man (it is remarkable how many managers think they can run an operation successfully without paying attention to the numbers) and, confronted with the evidence both on paper and physically, agrees to a simple inventory reduction plan and a set of controls to prevent future buying of excess stock.

LESSONS

A. *The MD has ignored the intrinsic warnings in his management reports. There is no point in having management information if you don't read it and act upon it.*

B. *He has failed to recognise what his eyes should have told him. A weekly (preferably daily) walk around the factory, discussing with* *the production staff the current progress and problems would have alerted him to the fact that there was a lot of idle hardware around the premises. Fortunately the Group Financial Director was alert to the signs when he visited the factory shortly after being appointed. In a few minutes he observed what the local manager had failed to observe in many months.*

5. BEHIND THE (FORMER) IRON CURTAIN

The Institute of Chartered Accountants of Scotland (ICAS), despite its local name, spreads itself around the world, as Scots people in general do. Reynard (all names in this book are fictitious), a former colleague of mine, who is at this time working for ICAS, has set up a series of one-week programmes in Kyiv (in the west of Ukraine) and Donetsk (in the east thereof) to acquaint university lecturers with the basics of western accounting.

The first shock is the state of dereliction of the universities themselves. There clearly has not been any maintenance for years, and you never have to ask where the toilets are; you just follow your nose. The second shock is that the delegates themselves are the opposite; smartly (but not expensively) dressed, very proper in attitude, very welcoming and very keen to learn.

Another shock is in their speech patterns. In all the Cold War movies made in the west, the Soviet agents spoke very slow, stilted, pompous English, which became the accepted norm. However, listening to the class chattering, I feel as if I'm hearing a group of Italians; the speech is lively and musical, with many highs and lows. So when I speak the few Russian phrases which I've taught myself beforehand, I do it with a hammy Italian accent and they're suitably impressed. Nyet problem!

The third shock is in discovering how programmed they are. When I seek to raise some discussion in the group by asking how they would decide on the level of advertising spend, a delegate at the back of the class stands up, says "Advertising will be one and one half per cent of turnover" and sits down again. The entire class then claps; he has given the official textbook answer! This means that we shall have to teach largely by discussion; merely telling them about capitalist practices is not going to get through to them without everyone joining in the discussion and learning "why" as well as "what".

The fourth shock is the best of all; our contact man and main translator is an ex-KGB colonel, whom I shall call "Andrei". He is the most cultured, professional, intelligent, diligent person with whom I've ever worked... quite unlike his former employers.

We do have to educate him on one matter, though. Each morning when he meets us he opens with a gem such as "Last night at a speech in the Guildhall the British Chancellor of the Exchequer said..." and we have to explain to him that the British have no interest in politics whatsoever, but we would like to know the football and cricket scores if he could oblige. So we duly get "Last night Aberdeen were beaten 2-1 by Werder Bremen but go through on the away goals rule" and he even masters the vagaries of cricket scores with a little help. More about him later.

The subject of football comes closer when we are invited to watch a European Cup tie between Dynamo Kyiv and Paris Saint-Germain. The stadium is a vast concrete bowl without a roof, and the temperature is at a bone-chilling level, a long, long way below zero. As the Kyiv team run out on to the park, the air is suddenly filled with large pieces of confetti, which are kept afloat for a considerable time by the warmer air rising from the crowd. Eventually the thousands of pieces settle on the crowd and on the pitch itself.

We ask our host about this strange custom. He explains that the pieces are in fact banknotes, from the previous currency which became worthless as a result of hyper-inflation, and was replaced by a new, larger currency unit. It dawns horribly that what we are teaching our classes about keeping their working capital low may have no relevance here. If you are in an era of very high inflation, the usual low working capital dictum does not apply... as soon as you receive any money from a customer you must buy more stock before the prices go up any further. Fortunately, we're told, the new currency is reportedly more stable and that has ceased to be necessary.

The programme runs over several months of week-long visits, with a wide range of presenters covering the main topics of Western accounting, and providing copious notes and examples. Predictably, the understanding of the Ukrainians varies greatly according to their previous learning and occupations, and the translators have to work long hard days without respite, their reactions on a knife-edge.

Occasionally one of the presenters uses a Russian expression they have learned, and the translator will immediately repeat it to the class in English, to the great amusement of the class. At the end of every day the translators are utterly drained from the constant effort of listening closely to every single word of the day.

My second module is five weeks later and I return home with a deep tan, as the temperature in Donetsk is by then +25ºC and we work afternoons and evenings, with the mornings spent sunbathing by the lake in the park. My colleagues from the earlier winter modules are not amused.

Kyiv was (and I hope still is, despite its many troubles) an impressive city in the centre, with a variety of complementary architectural styles. Donetsk, on the other hand, is a rough-and-ready industrial city, the only sign of culture being a vast selection of paintings on display in the main streets, some of the artwork very impressive. The prices being asked for the paintings are embarrassingly low, an indication of the very limited financial resources of the population at the time. Although I'm no art collector, I'm struck by the immediacy and vibrancy of their paintings, quite unlike anything I've seen in the west, and now have several of them at home.

ICAS has given us good basic learning material to provide the students, and our discussions with them reveal further needs which we promise to meet on our next visit (see chapter 9).

LESSONS

A. *Given that this is a unique project in so many respects, it is hard to come out from it with any conventional learning points for businesses. For me, the most important learning point (fortunately picked up at the very beginning) is not to assume that **anything** in such different economic, social and cultural circumstances is similar to what I'm accustomed to.*

The hyperinflation is a good example, but there are many

less obvious ones, such as perennial shortages of fuel and other commodities, which completely reverse the normal business maxim of running on low inventory. In any area of pronounced economic or social upheaval, you must adjust your working methods to the local circumstances, even if it goes against all of your training and your favoured modus operandi.

B. *In an area of very different social conditions from those to which you are accustomed, you need to recognise that people's aspirations and understanding are very different (sometimes diametrically so) and you have to amend your management and communication methods accordingly. That is easy to say in a paragraph, but difficult to do in practice without a period of learning and adaptation. Stay very alert and use simple, unequivocal words.*

C. *This is a very personal learning point: difficult though it is, I try not to give our pupils any false hope for an immediately brighter future. Now as I write this, Donetsk is in turmoil... I hope they find peace in the near future.*

6. STATIONERY BUT NOT STATIONARY

The group financial director from project 1 is now installed as financial director of a larger group involved in printing, stationery and related products, and calls me about the business stationery products subsidiary in his group. Could I speak to the subsidiary's very go-ahead managing director about providing some training for the sales force? Sounds like fun.

The MD proves to be the ideal client, knowing exactly where and how he wants his business to go and having a clear idea of what he needs to get there. His immediate objective is to give his sales force a better appreciation of the commercial parameters of a business (i.e. any business) so that they can be more effective in selling their business stationery.

Having already run such courses in the window group (chapter 1) I can run one at very short notice, but what about some additional training in the use of business stationery? For example, if a customer wants 3-part delivery notes printed, can the sales person convince the customer that he should have 4-part delivery notes? To do that, the sales person will have to understand the systematic purposes and mechanics of the various documents which the company designs and prints. The MD recognises the benefits of that stream of training, and we agree on a 2-day course: a day on the financial performance and control of a business, and a day on the documents needed to operate that business effectively.

The business finance day comprises 4 sections:

- understanding the profit statement, especially the relationship of variable costs to fixed costs and the fact that margins, which are the real revenue of any business, are much more important than sales (a constant theme!)

- understanding a balance sheet by building one via 12 transactions in columns on a landscape A4 sheet
- understanding cash flow, using a worked example which appears to generate cash when you read it, but which goes heavily into the red when you calculate it over several periods even though you are making a profit
- considering all of the ways in which the main accounting systems can be by-passed or distorted, and understanding how the company's stationery products, if properly used, can prevent these problems from occurring, accidentally or deliberately, in their customers' businesses

The sales team are a very alert group, which results in a lively two days, after which the team are confident that they can considerably improve their sales performance. As it happens, I catch sight of the MD a few years later when I pull in off the motorway for a coffee, and he is well satisfied with the subsequent improvement in performance of his sales force.

Feelgood factor 10.

LESSONS

A. *It doesn't matter whether a business is selling stationery, machinery, electrical goods or patent medicine; the principles and financial dynamics are the same, and therefore the same course material can be used with a minimum of modification.*

B. *A sales team is the group of people most seen by the customers. The team or the individual salespersons themselves are therefore the customers' vision (sometimes their entire vision) of the company and hence the team must have the best possible range of weapons in their armoury.*

It is therefore not just a matter of possessing selling skills; the sales team must have a full understanding of how their products benefit their customers, and must be able to demonstrate these benefits clearly to the customers. In this particular case, the sales force are NOT selling business stationery; they are selling their customers a better-controlled and therefore more profitable business, through more precise documentary control.

I have been astonished at the number of companies whose management regard the sales force as the necessary evil – the salespersons are both the front line soldiers and the company image!

7. HEAD OFFICE PROCEDURES

A former colleague has moved ahead by leaps and bounds and is now the chief financial officer of a sizeable finance company. He has not had adequate time to examine the detailed workings of his head office finance department, and although they appear to be functioning smoothly, he wants me to carry out a review of their procedures and controls to give him the necessary reassurance.

His finance department are a young and lively bunch, and the feeling upon walking in the door is positive (not that one's initial impression is 100% reliable; there are occasional surprises in either direction, but they don't occur here). The department lives up to the good initial impression it creates, and after three days I give him a note of various relatively minor issues which need tightening up.

What I fail to do is to point out in my short report that none of the revealed defects is serious, and that the department is in good shape overall in terms of both structure and performance. So instead of being praised, my unfortunate ex-colleague who has been doing such an efficient job gets a mild roasting from his boss when the boss reads the reports.

LESSONS

A. *This is a bad omission on my part, the sloppiness almost certainly being caused by the fact that it was an easy project. Be very wary of anything "easy"; it can make you less attentive. Because you're not in a battle, you have to make an extra effort to be at the top of your game.*

B. *On most types of instructor course, be they military or civilian,* *you will be told to give praise before giving criticism (and it is usually appropriate to repeat the praise after the criticism, except where the criticism is severe). Rather than just reporting the items needing improvement, I should have begun my report with an overall summary pointing out that the department was functioning well overall, with only a few minor improvements needed.*

Black mark.

8. WORLDWIDE MACHINERY

An English company is making high-quality industrial power units (some standard, some custom-built) for sale worldwide. These range from portable items such as the small mobile units on standby for starting aircraft engines to large non-mobile units such as the massive built-in generators used as emergency standby for institutions such as hospitals. Remarkably, the company does not have a contract costing system; moreover, a few other controls which one would normally regard as essential are missing.

The financial director is newly appointed and he wants this fixed... fast. Just how fast is indicated by the fact that he hires me despite my never having designed such a system. He does have a secret weapon available, however, a resourceful IT lady who knows everything that moves in the factory. Just as importantly, she has a full understanding of human nature. Together we map out the purchasing system, which is conventional, but not complete. In some cases, components are bought for general stock, and in others they are bought for specific projects.

The remedy is a simple flowchart, which we do on Lotus 1-2-3 (remember that?) in the absence of any other tools. In fact, you can use any spreadsheet for flowcharting if you set the column width to match the row height, thus giving you a squared background. Our approach is to set out what the system ought to be, and then identify the gaps. I need not bore the reader with the details, as they are entirely straightforward and conventional. In short, the goods do not go on system until they are actually in inventory. Instead, each item ordered should be allocated to a particular generator under construction, or about to be constructed per a build order, giving a trail from the outset.

This is a very straightforward project, especially since the IT lady knows every potential glitch in the book, and once we have agreed the structure she builds the system to the letter. What's more, it works from the moment it is started.

There is, however, an entirely different and damaging issue which I discover in mapping out the requirements. The company has three streams of product and each stream is classified as a business group, in the charge of a manager assigned to that group only. Each manager is awarded a bonus which depends on the on-time completion of each order. An order for a large custom-built product takes about 9 months to be completed in the factory.

However, there is a fourth group: the installation team, who ship each product to the customer anywhere in the world, and who instal the product on site for the customer. The typical time for a large installation is 5 weeks. If the product is 2 weeks late from the factory after 40 weeks of building time, the factory manager involved loses only a small part of his completion bonus. Moreover, the product occasionally lacks a few peripheral items, electrical connexions being a common example. Sometimes items are taped to the product instead of being properly fitted.

But... because the factory completion is 2 weeks late, the installation manager has therefore only 3 weeks instead of 5 weeks to complete the installation, and he has to acquire the missing items as well. He ends up half-way around the world, buying components at disadvantageous prices, not to mention express delivery, hiring additional local labour (often not familiar with the product) at overtime rates, and working around the clock to meet the completion deadline. Moreover, all of this incompetence is paraded on the client site through no fault of his own.

However, the costing systems show that the factory managers have achieved 98-99% of their target, and the installation manager has missed his targets continually by a huge percentage. The factory managers get most of their bonus and the installation manager, who is the hardest-working and most organised of them all, is the company's whipping-boy.

I report this to the financial director, who fully accepts that a change is urgently needed, but the managing director refuses to change the arrangements for the (irrelevant) reason that the existing bonus system has only just been launched with a big fanfare. Yes, he may look a bit stupid if he changes the bonus scheme shortly after it has been launched, but he will look a lot worse if the company continues to blow away margin on unfinished products. However, I realise that I'm not going to get through to him.

Fortunately the company is sold shortly thereafter and the new owners are able to deal with the problem once we explain it to them.

LESSONS

A. *Irrefutable.* **Drysdale's First Law of Systems** *is simple: IF PEOPLE CAN PASS ON PAIN, THEY WILL (not necessarily deliberately).*

Therefore all systems must be organised so that anyone attempting to pass on problems downstream, knowingly or otherwise, will suffer immediately.

In this case, each of the three manufacturing managers should have been responsible for their products all the way to final acceptance by the customers. The installation and commissioning team should have to be booked well in advance, to an exact date, with a penalty against the manufacturing team for any late submission of products for the installation and commissioning process.

Brutal, but simple and necessary.

B. *The bonus system would be better termed "completion pay" or something similar, so that it would be regarded as part of the essential process stream, instead of being some kind of perk. My usual preference is "performance pay" because the word "performance" places a clear onus on the employees if they wish to earn the rewards.*

9. UKRAINE AGAIN

This is merely a later phase in the programme described in part 5, the main difference being that having made a previous trip we are much better prepared to meet the needs of our audiences. I bring our ex-KGB contact man Andrei some children's books including a Beatrix Potter compendium for his grandchildren, whom he is teaching English, and he is delighted. Such material is scarce in the former Soviet Union at the time of this project.

At the end of the trip he takes my colleague and me to a high promontory overlooking the Dnieper, which at that stretch is so wide that it appears to be a large lake. Amongst the displays up there is an open-air museum of former Soviet military hardware, and especially military aircraft, in their traditional drab green camouflage. He seems intrigued that I can name them all, and when we come to a twin-engined transport, I say "Lisunov Li-2".

He looks at me quizzically and says "Everybody knows that is a Douglas Dakota."

"Made under licence in the Soviet Union" I reply. "You can tell by the engine intakes."

I'm wearing a sweatshirt bearing the sports brand name Lonsdale, and he looks at me searchingly and says quietly "Lonsdale was a spy."

I'm taken aback for a moment, and then I remember.

"Of course... Gordon Lonsdale! He and his wife worked for the Admiralty."

"No," he replies, deadpan, "They worked for us."

I fall about laughing... Andrei, wherever you are, I hope all is well with you.

LESSONS

A. *You can't fool the KGB.*

B. *I should have asked him about Buster Crabb.*

PART 2

THE LATER DAYS:
HELL BREAKS LOOSE

10. YORKIE PORKIES (THINGS GET NASTY)

At last... what I've been looking for: a permanent group financial director role based in Yorkshire, within weekly commuting distance of home. Plenty to get the teeth into: a recent major acquisition, various activities being spun out to separate subsidiaries, a massive factory expansion, some new state-of-the-art plant and presumably some organisation work to be done.

The main company has acquired another company in the same manufacturing business and there is a major project in process to extend the factory and bring most of the equipment of the acquired company to the site of the main company. Given that the acquired company is based a considerable distance away and is of similar size to the acquiring company, it is a complex exercise, both logistically and on paper. Trade must continue during the move.

The main company also has two smaller related activities, which it has located separately. I ask the reader to bear with me for not naming the precise industry involved, for delicate reasons which will become apparent. Let's just say that we're supplying the construction industry.

The initial financial to-do list is predictably extensive, the main concern being to get all the various locations producing rapid, reliable and relevant monthly operating accounts, and acting on them. Luckily, the acquired company has come from a well-controlled group and the other two subsidiaries are not complex, so a substantial and informative monthly financial pack can be produced rapidly, the critical path being, as usual, a reliable monthly stock-count at each location. So few companies have perpetual inventory records.

Because of the considerable amount of additional funding required to double the size of the group, the finance costs will be heavy, which places extensive pressure on the newly-formed group to perform on or over budget from the outset... and that does not happen. There are the usual explanations: late delivery of new machinery, the transfer of production equipment from the purchased company to the main site taking longer than anticipated, et cetera. However, a high proportion of such projects go over budget and over timescale, so it isn't exactly new territory. Not acceptable, but still manageable.

I have arrived in month 11 of the financial year of the acquisition, and in reviewing the results and working papers of month 10 I note that the "month" has included 2 days of month 11. Such a ruse, in addition to bordering on fraud, is self-defeating, because it means that in the following month the business has to achieve the same output in 4 fewer days than have been included in the current month. That never happens when people play that game, but I decide not to say anything until I become familiar with the group's numbers. Nevertheless, a little red light is blinking.

With the financial year-end not far away I look through the company accountant's working papers and identify two miscellaneous receivables that do not appear to be, er, receivable. That will have to be dealt with at the year-end, only weeks away. But there are more pressing issues: instead of a single unit we are now several units, each with a full individual accounting requirement, and these need to be fully set up for the forthcoming year, so my attention turns of necessity to getting those in train.

The auditors, from a major national firm, duly arrive and I query with them the two miscellaneous "assets" which do not appear to be recoverable. The audit partner looks highly embarrassed and mumbles "I think we should just leave those items in for the time being." He is clearly uncomfortable.

So... a consultant from the audit firm has been deeply involved in the document which raised the finance for the expansion, and here are two valueless current assets which the audit partner does not wish to remove.

Hmmm.

This causes me to take an even closer look at the rest of the balance sheet than I might otherwise have done. Would you believe it; I find an asset recorded three times in the balance sheet... once as a fixed asset, once as an item of inventory and once as an amount receivable. Unfortunately the audit has been "completed" (I use the term loosely) before I make that discovery. The company's accountant clearly isn't the type of person to make spurious entries, so the instructions must have come from the highest level.

What next? We have a good business (albeit with some strange accounting) which has just acquired another good business of the same type. If the profit projections are reasonably realistic, there could perhaps be sufficient profit by the end of the first year of expansion to eliminate these quirks and still show a passable result. The moral issue is that the acquired company has been closed down, resulting in around 200 redundancies which with families included will be about 500 people without any income in an area which is not thriving... but it is much too late to change that.

I decide to keep my own counsel for the time being and concentrate on the next financial year, which is imminent. The management accountant and I produce a copiously detailed draft budget which comes in well below the business plan profit, and the managing director helps me prune it until the target figures look both sensible, and perhaps still achievable. Some managerial staff are dispensed with at this point as part of the cost reduction. Our audit is signed off and I can turn my attention fully to the financial performance of the group as a whole.

Of course, it doesn't work. The company goes off-budget immediately and stays that way, the gap widening monthly. The young representative from the three financing banks comes to see us after the first quarter's results, which are not inspiring. I have told both the managing director and the production director to have their stories well prepared, but in the event both of them fail to come up with either a satisfactory explanation for the poor result, or a plan for improving it. Interestingly the banker turns to me and says of the situation "This result is down to you, Alasdair"... an intriguing view, considering that I neither make nor sell the product, but I keep quiet nevertheless.

When he has gone I give the other two executive directors a very large piece of my mind for hanging me out to dry. I had warned them that they would need to be on top of their game for the bank meeting, but they have performed like a pair of dumbstruck schoolboys, unable to give any reason for the performance, nor any sign of any initiative to improve it.

Over the first quarter I have found a few other interesting accounting treatments from the previous year, which when added to the other anomalies mean that the acquiring company did not achieve anything like the previous year's profit which it claimed... and yet it passed the annual audit.

At the next board meeting the managing director has failed to follow up a requirement stated by me and endorsed by the chairman to liquidate some non-commercial assets to improve the cash position. That is the final straw.

After the meeting the main non-executive director, representing the external finance providers, is using my office to make a phone call and when he has finished I lay on the desk a large folder with the evidence that the whole expansion project is based on an apparent trading performance that has not been achieved in reality, but is derived from 7 separate accounting frauds, which have clearly been perpetrated at the top level before my arrival. Moreover, they should have been identified easily by the auditors, who had supplied the "consultant" who assisted with the business plan.

The non-exec must have had an interesting train journey back to London with the chairman, who phones me in a very different tone from his usual lofty mien. He is both sympathetic and conciliatory, and he very quickly lays down the terms of my departure from the company, an exit route which will leave him in charge of politicking his way through the inevitable fallout. I take legal advice from my professional institute to ensure that I am not breaking any law in meeting the terms of my departure.

I also pass on a message to the fraud squad regarding an entirely different matter which I have noted in the group's transactions in Europe (I was once speaking at a conference alongside the Inland Revenue's head of fraud, who gave me her business card). The fraud squad advise me later that they are taking that matter seriously and I leave it in their hands. The trail points towards a small land-locked country.

The wayward MD is demoted and coincidentally is later replaced by the MD of one of my previous clients. It's a very small world! Some months later the replacement MD and I have a useful conversation over lunch, and I'm glad to hear that the guilty parties have been suitably dealt with. In writing this account, I have checked that the company still exists two decades later, producing genuine quality products under different ownership.

That's good news. It deserved to succeed, even if some of its leaders didn't.

LESSONS

A. *Where do I begin? The chairman and MD came across very well at the recruitment interview, and both were well-known in their industry, as were their professional advisors, financial and legal. Moreover, I asked an appropriate range of questions which were answered specifically, so I don't think there was anything which should have alerted me to the realities. I'm not even sure how much, if anything, the chairman knew. I therefore conclude that I handled the interview as well as I could have, and that I shouldn't have been smelling a rat at that stage.*

B. *When dealing with overbearing people, you often have only a second or two to react. At my first board meeting, I was summarising the financial performance by presenting my prepared summary, and when asked a question by the chairman, I consulted another schedule beyond the summary before answering the question. At that point the chairman, who was rather obsessed by his classical chairman role, said "I do like a financial director who can answer questions without having to look up the numbers."*

I looked him in the eye and said, deadpan: "So do I, Chairman. So do I."

He should have concluded from that response that I had issues bubbling under the surface, but instead he continued grandstanding in front of the rest of the board. There is a fine line between being authoritative and being domineering, and he was clearly beyond the line. In such circumstances you usually have only two approaches: smile and bear it without flinching, or meet it head on. I think the latter approach was the right one for the circumstances and I gave as good as I got, and he subsequently softened his approach.

C. *It is a well-known phenomenon amongst financial executives that in some businesses when financial results are good, the operational management are deemed to have done well, and when the results are poor it is somehow the fault of the financial leaders. This group was one such business.*

However, in many other businesses in which I have worked, the operational directors have fully accepted the responsibility for the operating results, whatever they have been. This was my first taste of something different.

11. DRASTIC PLASTIC

A long-time buddy, both socially and professionally, in darkest Englandshire calls to see if I would examine his inventory and production records, which are giving him divergent inventory figures. A good little exercise, but I'm beginning to wonder if I will ever get out of the world of plastics. I follow all the trails through the production and accounting records and emerge with book figures that almost exactly match the production records. I even turn up unannounced at a stock count on the night shift, but it's all well-ordered.

The only debatable factor is a very large hopper full of plastic pellets, which are the raw material for melting down into plastic products. You can tell roughly how full the hopper is by tapping on the side; the point at which the sound changes from a dull noise to a clang indicates the level. However, the meniscus could be convex or concave according to whether the last movement was of pellets in or pellets out. But if we assume that the top of the pellets is neither convex nor concave, any error factor will be of no importance in relation to the total stock of material.

Neither of us is entirely convinced that the numbers are square, so we go through the entire trail together and the figures still match.

Nothing more to do.

LESSONS

A. *The controller was right to call in some help, because sometimes you just need a fresh pair of eyes to look at something which is baffling you. A similar situation occurred at the end of project 33, when I was the one who couldn't make the numbers tally.*

12. GODZILLA IN MANILA

The problem with this particular story is that, as with the others, it's all true. Nobody in her or his right mind will believe it, but I have recorded it exactly as it happened, and for reasons which will become apparent, that will be a little hard to swallow. But please try.

When I arrive home from the drastic plastic reconciliation, my wife tells me "Sven called. Guess where you're going next."

"Singapore?" I suggest hopefully. You can always dream. Sven does handle some faraway locations.

"Close," she replies, "Manila". Actually it's a long way north-east of Singapore, but it doesn't look that far on the small-scale world map in my diary. Good; not only do I need a break from plastic companies, but I'm beginning to feel the same about the UK in general.

I'm told that I've been booked in to a specific hotel on arrival in Manila and someone will pick me up the next morning and take me to the boss's house. When he arrives, the driver tells me to take my swimming gear, a request which seems a little strange until I realise that it's Sunday, which is barbecue day in any civilised country. Good timing, Drysdale. It's a handy way to meet the management team, most of whom appear to be Welsh. A permanent financial controller has been recruited, but is obliged to work his notice period on his current job, and will arrive from the UK in about four months' time. Pool, sunshine, good company, good beer... good start.

Monday... down (and then up) to business. The office in the city is on the 10th floor of a tower block on Ayala Triangle in the heart of Metro Manila, and it's a busy place. The apartment they have arranged for me is on the 12th floor of a twin-tower block just across the triangle from the office, and they've made a reasonable job of patching up the bullet-holes from the last attempted coup. Oh, yes, and Imelda Marcos is living in an apartment just around the corner, together with her shoes. Neat.

After a few days I confess to the boss that I think I am the only male in the world to suffer from morning sickness, but he assures me that it's only the elevator, which has a strange, unpleasant swaying motion. Apparently, I'm not alone in my ailment; others have similar trouble with their semi-circular canals and start their working days feeling somewhat queasy.

Filipinos and more specifically Filipinas are amongst the liveliest people on the planet, and they make a welcome change from some of the more serious westerners. The financial controller is a diminutive girl of Chinese descent who is very much the boss, and the whole department is noisy with frequent laughter, which is a good sign. Raoul, the only male on the team, is quiet by comparison, and sits in the far corner with a serious expression. The year is 1995, modern computers are still in their infancy and the team have built themselves an entire accounting system on Lotus 1-2-3. The Philippine peso is a small currency unit, so the numbers are large, and the carrying capacity of the floppy disks isn't.

The company makes garments for department stores, using raw material mainly bought from Korea in US dollars, and all local costs of manufacture, shipping and administration are in Philippine pesos. The goods are shipped to Hong Kong, who pay in HK dollars, and then forwarded to the UK, who pay in Sterling. As a method of preventing anybody from knowing what genuine margin the business is making at any level, it's world-class.

Other than running the finance department, which runs itself, my only responsibility is to prepare the budget for the following year, which starts on 1st January, and we are already into November. As Lotus 1-2-3 at that time offers only a single sheet, the budget involves hundreds of rows and scores of columns and corresponding check-totals to cover all the currencies involved. Good fun, and a welcome activity, given that the finance department runs without any input from me. They work a 10-hour day, or more if there's a flap on the go.

The company has two factories, one in an industrial area called Cavite (three syllables) on the outskirts of Manila and the other on Mactan Island, linked by a bridge to the larger island of Cebu, a popular holiday destination for Japanese and other nationalities. The Cavite factory is being targeted by the KMU (Kilusang Mayo Uno, the communist First of May Movement, not to be confused in any way with the Kuomintang, or KMT, who are of the opposite persuasion).

Garments are being sabotaged, and the company has surreptitiously changed its gate guards from paperwork guards to real gunslinging guards, mostly ex-commandos who now work as security agents. Their paperwork is no match for that of the regular guards, and causes a few documentary hiccups. Ho-hum.

Our personnel manager receives a death threat from the KMU, and hastily departs to another job in another company. Things are hotting up. She is the last "personnel manager" with whom I work; all of the subsequent ones I encounter anywhere go by the ridiculous title of "human resources manager", a term of extraordinary pomposity, doubtless invented by some consultant.

The boss gets professional about security. Cars, drivers and journey times are changed every day, so that nobody external can work out a pattern for an ambush. Matters are brought into sharp relief when the manager of the factory adjacent to ours in Cavite is assassinated at the traffic lights near the industrial estate. A couple of bullets whip past the boss's guarded house one night. Things are a bit quieter on Ayala Triangle, fortunately for me, but we keep a loaded Smith & Wesson in the glove compartment of the company car just in case...

In the second week, just when I'm starting to get somewhere with the multi-currency budget, the commercial director suddenly appears and says "Typhoon. Everybody home". Nobody queries him. The entire complement of people shut down their PCs and disappear, and I wonder if they live in houses which will withstand the onslaught. Having only a short distance to go, I stay a little longer, then head for the apartment via a food shop. There are three categories of severity for typhoons, but this one is so severe that they give her a special category 4 and classify her as a super-typhoon. Her name is Angela, but angelic she isn't.

After a day and a half holed up in the apartment and having consumed the snacks I bought and exhausted the limited variety of TV offerings, I decide that it's worth risking the 30-metre dash to the Swiss Restaurant at ground level to get some lunch and a beer. At the foot of my tower I pause to pick my moment and sprint for the restaurant, but as I'm running, two enormous plate glass sheets and a dustbin go sailing past me at head height. I choose my moment for the return journey much more carefully.

The typhoon eventually subsides, and as we resume work in the office, tales of the carnage begin to circulate, and a death toll in excess of 500 is reported. I ask the inane question as to why it's called a typhoon in the Pacific Ocean, a hurricane in the Atlantic Ocean and a cyclone in the Indian Ocean, but nobody knows, nor are they interested. Electric power is out for most of a week, so the elevators and air conditioning are hors de combat. By the time we make it to the 10th floor on foot we are (a) exhausted and (b) soaking wet with sweat. Inevitably, none of the computers or communication systems can be used so the boss sends everyone home very early each day.

I have some business to conduct with the Hong Kong office, so I head off on a Thursday. Coming into the old Kai Tak airport with the runway built out into the harbour, you were always bound to have a spectacular landing, whichever the direction. Approaching over the harbour, you could see the entire backdrop of skyscrapers reflected on the harbour water, and coming in the other way you would sashay down the glide path with skyscrapers, advertisement hoardings and lines of washing zipping past the wingtips.

Unfortunately there is no love lost between HK and Manila, so my Friday in the HK office is not very fruitful; luckily there is nothing critical under discussion. The administrator is terrified of Filipinos and in all his years with the company he has never visited Manila, being convinced that he will be kidnapped and sold into slavery. Or so they tell me in Manila.

On Saturday I treat myself to a train ride to Kwangchow (Guangzhou) in China. At the station a small, elderly but spry Burmese woman offers to show me the great city for a fixed fee in US dollars which will cover all fares and refreshments. I suspect a scam but she persists, and I decide to trust her.

Good move; I have a wonderful day and see far more of the city than I would otherwise have done. She knows the city intimately, but is very circumspect with her choice of words and several times stops to ask me "You're not a member of The Party, are you?" Her good command of English comes, she says, from having worked for the US military in some other unspecified country. A lucky find for me; I hope she has continued to avoid the Party for the rest of her days. Speaking of the Party, I notice that the architecture is very reminiscent of that on the outskirts of Kyiv. Draw your own conclusions.

When I get back to Manila from Hong Kong on Sunday evening, I'm just getting out of the taxi at my apartment block when the boss, who is an inveterate clubber, emerges with pals from RJ's night club in the basement.

"Hey, Al, we're all going to RJ's in Quezon City; you're coming, too."

"No way! I'm knackered and I'm on the 6 o'clock flight to Cebu in the morning."

But he won't take no for an answer and reluctantly I join them for the trip to RJ's club in Quezon City. RJ is Ramon Jacinto, a leading rock musician who owns several clubs which feature excellent live bands who are almost as good as the more famous acts whom they emulate. He also helps young talent develop, and looks after their early careers. Our "short trip" to his club in Quezon City turns into an all-nighter and I get half an hour's sleep in my apartment before heading off for Cebu airport and Mactan Island.

Unfortunately I am seated next to a Big 8 (as they were then) partner who insists on talking to me throughout the flight, and especially telling me how wonderful this new invention called "the internet" is, and how it will revolutionise the world. I argue strongly that it will just be another passing electronic fad, which more or less sums up my ability to keep abreast of technology. To my relief I escape from him when we land at Cebu and I'm met and taken across the bridge to Mactan Island.

I have a chat with the finance department there, to hear if they have any problems. Only one: can I build them a model on Lotus 1-2-3 that will convert everyone's monthly pay to the right number of each denomination of notes and coins automatically? The Philippine peso is a very small denomination of currency, so the payroll runs to vast numbers. Now that's a fun game, and after an hour or so we have a working cash breakdown model, tested with all manner of strange amounts. Whatever we do, the check-totals are all zero. Job done, and they steer me to a desk they have cleared for me in the middle of the main office.

Hong Kong, Guangzhou, RJ's, the flight, etc., are all too much, and my head sags gently until it rests on the desk, and I enter a deep, deep sleep in front of the entire office.

The Cebu boss calls up Manila on the radio (there are no telephones here). Who is this drunken idiot you've sent down here, setting a bad example to my staff? Leave him alone, growls the Manila boss; he was doing a great Mick Jagger impersonation at three o'clock this morning up in Quezon City. The Cebu boss relays this instruction to his staff and the situation is resolved; Filipinos respect a guy who can party and I am left in dreamless peace until a hand shakes my shoulder and a voice tells me it is lunch-time.

We walk (probably lurch in my case) down to a shaded jetty surrounded by small boats bobbing up and down gently as the fishermen mend their nets. Idyllic. Somebody places in front of me a hollowed-out pineapple full of pineapple juice and ice-cubes. I grab the straw and suck up a huge quantity of juice to slake the thirst I have developed, only to realise that I am drinking a very potent rum-and-pineapple cocktail. But I'm so thirsty I drink even more of it, and a very strange thing happens. My head clears, I feel wonderful, and for the rest of the day and at dinner in the evening I feel fit and well. Medical science cannot explain it, and I wish I had the recipe.

Back in Manila I'm updating the budget (somebody mentions a major change almost daily) when somebody asks what the finance department is doing for the Christmas party. Apparently each department has to put on a show of some kind. This wasn't in the brief for the job, but interim directors have to deal with such diversions, and enquiries reveal that Raoul is a fine guitarist. In addition to his own acoustic guitar he brings me a battered old round-hole with the D-string key jammed solid, so that we have to tune everything to that string. Filipinos are amongst the most musical people on earth, so we schedule a practice for after-office time to see what happens.

They respond immediately and harmoniously to a few warm-up numbers, the girls even doing the "such a lovely face" come-back lines from Hotel California without any prompting. But nobody can decide what we should sing, so eventually we write our own song about the company and its most prominent characters. It evolves over a couple of weeks (after hours, I stress; there are still versions 17 to 23 of the budget to be completed) and eventually we have a little three-chord rock 'n' roll number which sounds suspiciously like Chantilly Lace, but not to worry. It'll have to do.

Come the evening of the office Christmas party we are the first department to perform and the girls are on song from the first note. The other departmental acts follow and there is tension as the judges (the senior management team) score the teams. Great whoops of joy as we're announced the winners! We have to repeat the song, with even more gusto, and we're told that we will also be performing the song at the factory Christmas party. In the meantime, the finance department spend the rest of the evening discussing how they are going to spend the cash prize.

The factory's Christmas party is on Christmas Eve, out in Cavite, where so much of the political unrest and sabotage festers. The background is uncomfortable to say the least, but the Filipinos are very committed to their partying and no scabby political movement is going to get in the way of a Christmas wingding.

The stage is set near the factory's high boundary fence, and many of the turns are drag acts, mostly by the factory supervisors; the production manager is amazed to discover how many of his key men swing both ways. Beyond the factory fence is a grassy knoll from which someone is filming the entire proceedings with a movie camera which shines a powerful light. Grassy knolls have a decidedly dodgy track record, and on the previous night's TV there was a Kevin Costner movie in which a camera contained a gun, so we perform our song rather faster than we did in the office.

After that we spend a wonderful evening with the factory crew; one of them is an excellent guitarist and singer, and he trades songs with our lad Raoul, the girls chipping in with immaculate harmonies. Rock 'n' roll brings people together far better than governments do. Raoul is actually a classical player, but like any self-respecting Filipino, he can rock.

Before we know it, it is long past midnight and those of us based in the city pile into a Jeepney and head for Ayala Triangle in the city centre. We reach it at about one-thirty, when the traffic on the eight-lane comes to a complete halt. Despite the fact that we are now well into Christmas Day, the shops are still open in a blaze of light and the streets are heaving with people, most of them carrying clanking bottles. Nothing seems to be moving anywhere on the road, so we get out to investigate. A pregnant lady crossing the eight-lane has started to give birth, and without the remotest chance of an ambulance getting through the crowds, the baby is being delivered there and then on the tarmac with an audience of hundreds.

An enormous cheer goes up when the cry of the baby is heard, the next sound being the popping of champagne corks which were originally destined for celebrations later on Christmas Day. The baby is immediately and unanimously christened Ayala. As the crowd is clearly going to be around a long while we wish the van driver good luck, and hand him a large Christmas present before heading off on foot. Anywhere else in the world I would eventually wake up from this dream, but this is Manila and it's real.

Back to the budget. A newly-appointed group director visits from the UK and recoils in horror at the multiple-stage budget in its coat of many currencies. He readily agrees that we should do the whole exercise in one currency, which is what I'd argued for in the first place, and the exercise is rapidly completed, still complex but now much easier to assimilate.

Suddenly I'm surplus to requirements. The new local finance director for Manila is in the UK office being briefed, and I find myself on a plane heading eastwards (to complete a round-the-world journey) for a meeting with him. With me I take the lyrics of the finance department song and I warn him that he'd better be word-perfect by the time he hits Manila.

LESSONS (of a sort)

A. *Where do I begin? At first thought the only lesson one could relay about Manila is "Don't go there!" but you would be missing a lot if you by-passed it. In between the bullets it has a compelling rock'n'roll lifestyle. The rum is world-class, but be careful; despite its gentle demeanour it has a subsequent kick which is well outside the terms of the Geneva Conventions.*

B. *Umm... there are times in life when you just have to go with the flow, and others when you have to avoid the flow altogether. In Manila these come into stark relief and you often have to make your choice immediately. Nine times out of ten you will find yourself going with the flow unless you have a serious counter-revolutionary mission. Just enjoy it; one day these will be the good old days.*

C. *But if you have any kind of heart condition, forget it.*

13. MAN OF MYSTERY

For the life of me, I cannot remember this project. I have a vague memory of a group financial director who considered that one of his subsidiaries had too much inventory and/or was underperforming profit-wise, and that it was in medium-technology engineering. Not quite hi-tech, but certainly more than mere metal-bashing. While other projects remain clear in my memory in minute detail, this one refuses to resurface. Somewhere in the South of England, but where?

I don't think it was so awful that my memory has blotted it out; it is more likely that it was so mundane that it simply disappeared from consciousness. Sorry... but if it was that mundane, you wouldn't want to read about it anyway.

LESSONS

A. *Er... keep more detailed records of your activities.*

B. *In fact, let's expand a little. Around the turn of the century the UK Inland Revenue was getting tough with many people who were self-employed, contesting their tax returns and, I believe, their tax status. I made a point of keeping meticulous income and expenditure records and turned my details in to a firm of accountants for checking and presentation immediately after the end of each UK tax year. It was worth the fee, because I could sleep easily.*

14. HEAVY METAL... ON YOUR METTLE

Reynard calls.

Reynard moves in mysterious ways, as the cliché goes, but anyone less like a cliché probably doesn't exist. He also moves in mysterious places. He appeared unannounced during one of the Ukraine teaching sessions, and received a reception of which the Messiah would have been proud. He chomped the sheep's eyes with great relish in Kazakhstan. He turned up in what looked like army rugby kit in Edinburgh and slaughtered me at squash. And now he calls me and says he has an industrial project deep in Siberia.

For confidentiality I don't want to name the company or the industry.

The outfit concerned, which I shall call IvanCo, has been privatised for some time since the dissolution of the Soviet Union. Its shareholders include well-known industrial heavyweight groups from other countries and the Russian site is keen to adopt western management practices as rapidly as practicable; not just top management, but all levels from supervisors upwards. IvanCo is apparently the largest operation of its kind in the world, and wishes to hold its own with the best. (I note later that one of its competitors also claims to be the world's largest).

In some respects, the brief is easy; since the dawn of communism most people have done exactly what they were told if they are sensible, but from now on, every level of seniority will have to bear its appropriate share of responsibility and actually make decisions. A management training plan will have to cover nearly everything and everyone. If only it were that simple! Technical people will have to start considering commerciality instead of working to a given price structure, supervisory staff will have to think about safety and welfare, senior management will need to be concerned with public opinion and so on. Environmental issues will become an increasingly bigger part of everyone's life (we hope).

The timescale is relatively short, so there is a frenetic spell of drafting out a large matrix of the various levels of responsibility and the general categories of management and skills likely to be required at each level. I'm ready to go.

Being suddenly violently sick at Edinburgh Airport isn't a good start, but the recovery is surprisingly quick and I'm only slightly off-the-pace by the time we get to London. The connexion to Moscow is on time and in a few hours we are on the glide path down to Sheremetyevo... the throttles are suddenly pushed fully forward and after the usual slight lag the big jet surges forward and very steeply upward. As we level off at a higher altitude the skipper comes on the PA and says "Sorry about that, Ladies and Gentlemen; there was something down there I didn't like". Years later I'm in the same situation on finals to Dubai and the captain does and says exactly the same thing.

In the Irish Bar at Sheremetyevo we meet our translator and two other Russians who will be reviewing other aspects of the client's operation. It is so tempting to test whether the Guinness in this airport is as good as it is elsewhere, but in view of my earlier brief debility, I go without. Our flight is called and we head off towards our next stop, and a few hours later we have landed in Siberia and are trundling along miles and miles of rough concrete in what appears to be a vast wasteland lined with warplanes. MiGs, Tupolevs, Ilyushins, Yakovlevs, Sukhois, Antonovs, you name it; they have it. As we pass them we note that the engine pods are mostly empty, but it must look very impressive from the point of view of US spy satellites passing above.

We are met by an appointed courier, but not by our baggage, not that we seriously expected to see it. The courier takes us into town to buy some Siberian underwear (itchy) and we're ready for our onward journey. A Yak-40 transports us along with several crates of hens on the final leg and the tough little jet affords us a good view of the vast snow-covered terrain. A mini-bus meets us and takes us down a road from which there is no view; the snow is a few metres high on either side of the road, which is more like a giant ditch. We stay overnight very comfortably in what appears to be a company hostel.

The next morning we're taken to the gigantic factory of IvanCo, and in the vast offices we meet the senior director present, exact designation uncertain, but he appears to be at least the managing director, if not the chief executive. Our conversation is brief; his main thrust is that he is happy with the way the directors are performing and therefore we can consult from the next level downwards. No surprises there. We are taken to the office in which we shall be working, and the two male Russians we met at Moscow head off to do their (unspecified) technical work.

We review the list we have been given of interviewees at all levels of seniority. The plan is that each interview lasts 30 minutes, but that is untenable. Given that each change-over and introduction will take 10 minutes, that will leave 10 minutes for talk in Russian, and 10 minutes in English. Moreover, our poor translator is in need of frequent toilet breaks (nevertheless, she puts in a sterling performance throughout).

We decide that we will do 1-hour sessions, which after 10-minute changeovers will give us 25 minutes each in Russian and English, enough to give us sufficient appreciation of each interviewee's responsibilities and concerns... but of course that will mean that we shall only interview half of the number of employees originally selected. Not a problem; we shall eliminate every second level and still cover the full range of seniority.

. . . or so we think. Many of these people have probably never been asked for their uninhibited opinions before, and even the most carefully-phrased questions send them off into long tirades on subjects which, although relevant to their work and responsibilities, are not giving us the information we require. Moreover, some of the interviewees are giving us the answers they think we want to hear, rather than the stark realities. They are certainly not going to criticise the organisation. However, we begin to gain momentum.

Lunch... we are pleasantly surprised to find ourselves taken into a large canteen full of manual and clerical workers, and are impressed that the senior management eats democratically with all the other levels of staff. But it doesn't happen; an almost-invisible door opens in the far wall and we step into an opulent dining room for a meal which would cost a considerable amount in any western restaurant. Wine, vodka, beer and possibly other drinks are expected to be consumed over lunch. I stick with the beer.

After lunch we try new lines of questioning. "What changes would you like to see to improve your job"? Or even "what three changes"?

Bit by bit we make some progress by varying our tactics, and start to elicit some information, but it's hard going, and the end of the working day is very welcome.

Another problem is that few, if any, of the interviewees have ever thought much beyond their immediate tasks. Moreover, in the days of the Soviet Union, it wasn't usually a good move to express opinions that weren't exactly in keeping with the party line, or in this case, the company line. Cultures generally do not change overnight, except at very senior (i.e. political) level.

Day 2 therefore continues along the same lines as Day 1, although the quality of the interviews increases slightly through our increased familiarity with how the interviewees respond to different types of question, and to the ways in which the questions are phrased. But as a fact-finding process, it isn't doing very well. I tell my colleagues not to worry, as we shall be recommending what should be happening rather than what is actually happening. Nevertheless, the process doesn't make for a confident feeling.

We are invited to dinner in the company sauna for the evening, and our poor beleaguered translator gladly cuts out. After an initial greeting of vodka in the dining area we change and go through to the sauna itself. There is a round pool of perhaps 2 metres diameter, containing water of 1½ metres depth, the surface being about 2 metres below floor level. We are presumably to descend by the ladder fixed to the side of the pool, and our hosts will enjoy our excruciating pain as we tentatively enter the almost-freezing water.

No way! I tuck up into a ball and jump in from the top, the big splash soaking the onlookers and preventing them from seeing my huge intake of breath on hitting the icy water. Reynard follows suit with even more attitude and we cheerfully call to our hosts to come and join us. Come in; the water's lovely!!! This is not how it's meant to be, so they take their revenge in the hot room when they beat us enthusiastically with birch branches but we manage to keep chatting through the whole process. When we're dressed again an excellent meal appears out of apparently nowhere. Thus begins and ends my entire experience with saunas; Reynard as always is supremely unruffled and our Russian hosts are very entertaining company over dinner.

Day 3 is marginally better, but still not a mine of information. One of the interviewees, the transport co-ordinator, even goes down on his knees and clasps his hands in prayer to promise us "anything" if we can improve his job. Worry not, I assure the others; the training programme will write itself. We wind up our interviews, commit to a timetable for production and submission of the training programme and head for the airport.

I promise to have the training programme with Reynard within a short time, and that does not prove to be a problem. What we need is 10-12 columns for the various levels of seniority, a list of training requirements for every activity from acquisition of materials to shipping of products and collection of cash, and a narrative summary of how the training should be implemented.

The management and other functions are classified vertically from initial market research and design, to marketing and selling, order receipt and through to production, health & safety, inventory, sales and international cash collection, with side-issues such as pollution control. The main sections are broken into sub-sections, each containing the relevant business activities.

Across the top of each sheet, the seniority headings range from corporate management down through activity management and supervision, down finally to operatives and related staff. This gives a matrix of several thousand training requirements, each cell being filled with the number of hours envisaged as needed to bring the business from its recent state-owned status to a fully-fledged commercial enterprise. Several pages of narrative instruction explain how the programme is to be operated.

This comes as a shock to people whose culture has caused them to expect a very large bound book with a few hundred pages, but after some discussion IvanCo agree that the 12-page report does in fact cover all of the requirements. Every question they ask is answered.

And my missing luggage returns to me. It always does, because it looks scruffy and is never locked. Smart luggage which is locked sends out a message: "Steal me, steal me!" and people are surprised when it goes astray.

LESSONS

A. *This is even harder than Manila. For a start, always carry at least some clothes in your cabin baggage, so that you're self-sufficient if your hold baggage goes walkabout. Siberian underpants are not recommended.*

B. *Lost baggage – always learn the most important local travel words in the language of the country you are visiting. Listen carefully to the way any of the locals speak English, and copy that accent when you attempt their language.*

C. *Where you have a lot of information to impart to a client, consider whether a matrix or other graphic presentation will cut down the amount of verbiage; a matrix is the easiest form to write and to read. The one drawback is that it looks a lot less substantial than a cumbersome all-narrative report, and it can make the client believe that he isn't getting much for his money. In that case, challenge him to name any area that should be included in your report, and prove to him that the information is there, easy-to-find and quantified as well as identified.*

D. *Note to all aircraft freaks – Soviet (and now Russian) aircraft do NOT carry a CCCP registration. The code is SSSR... Svaz Sovětských Socialistických Republik, (Union of Soviet Socialist Republics), even though they're now just Russia. It just so happens that a Russian S looks like a C, and their R like a P. On dissolution of the Soviet Union, the other 14 republics had to go and get their own civil aircraft registration codes.*
    There; I feel much better for having got that off my chest.

E. *On the subject of lunch, I should have mentioned that Russian (and other Eastern European) beers are pretty damn good. Recommended.*

15. BACK TO BUILDING PRODUCTS

The large group that bought over our window group (see project no 1), and for whom I have worked at the head office for a period, is realising at last that it should dispose of several of its subsidiaries to their managing directors, and asks me to look at a couple of them.

The first one, in a part of the UK I have never before visited, is run by an elderly manager who is patently at the stage in life where retirement looms larger than any adventure. I cannot find any commercial, financial or personal stimulus to make him think otherwise. He is clearly tired after a long haul through his business life, and is making a sensible decision. He also has no second-in-command trained and capable of taking over, a common omission in the under-managed group which owns his company.

On an impulse, I spend a couple of hours driving around his area, looking at competitor companies, some of whose wares are prominently advertised. It becomes clear that whatever the reason, be it efficient production, better material or simply common commercial suicide, they are all selling similar products at little more than it costs my client to make them. He is making the right decision, and will feel greatly relieved when he is away from it all.

The other company up for disposal is in another part of the UK, and being run by a previous contact of mine, who clearly knows exactly what he is doing. His approach to buying out his subsidiary is hard-nosed and realistic, and I help him with the structure and narrative of his business plan, after which he is well on his way.

That ends my dealings with that large group, but it is worth reflecting on why they go into receivership a relatively short time later, so soon after being darlings of the investment community. The reason is quite simply that the group has grown entirely by acquisition of 90 owner-managed companies in similar industries. Why is that a dangerous method of growth? To answer that question, let us consider the psyche of the owner-managers who have built the individual businesses and eventually sold them to the group.

Being an owner-manager is one of the most demanding occupations on the planet. In addition to his family he (there was only one "she" in this particular group) is wedded to various other groups of people (employees, suppliers, customers, lenders, etc.) whose requirements are ever-present. The owner-manager lives and works at the beck and call of these other parties for years while he builds up his business, until a large group comes along and buys it. The transaction itself is an exhausting experience, and the former owner is locked into a 3, 4, or 5-year earn-out deal to obtain the agreed purchase price.

The manager has been running on adrenaline for years, or in some cases decades, so what do you think happens to his manic energy when he receives the final instalment of the purchase price for his business? It evaporates in a very short time. So the group for which I had worked had 90 businesses of which the great majority were psychologically over-the-hill concerns... run by once-aggressive businessmen who had run out of energy and were only going to go downwards.

I must confess to being wise after the event here, because although I had felt a general unease about the group's management when I worked for them I hadn't rationalised the very important psychological aspects of their business strategy of growth by acquisition. Moreover, if you have a few subsidiaries you can give them enough management attention to keep them sharp, but if you have over 90 of them, you have very little chance, even if you divide your group into divisions, which they did.

LESSONS

A. *The group in question has an emphatic hands-off policy regarding its subsidiaries. My enduring suspicion is that this is because the group management have very little (if any) know-how in terms of* *running a basic business. It is remarkably common for operational managers who rise to the level of group management to lose touch rapidly with the realities of their operating companies, to the point where they have a very limited range of constructive responses to any subsidiaries which encounter difficulties.*

B. *The group has therefore given no useful development advice to this particular subsidiary. It is aware of the age of the manager, but has made no effort to ensure that a suitable successor is identified and trained to take over the business. That particular circumstance is common throughout the group, whose philosophy was not to be involved with day-to-day management of the subsidiaries.*

C. *Growth by acquisition is NOT growth; it is merely change of ownership. The more growth is "bought" rather than reared, the less involvement the group management has in the operations, and therefore the less ability it has to stay ahead or even abreast of developments therein.*

D. *Overheads v sales is not a useful ratio. Overheads v net variable margin (or even gross margin) is a much more potent indicator of trend. Yet the group only tracks the overhead v sales ratio, which chugs along steadily, regardless of the fact that the gross margin is being steadily eroded. There is therefore no numerical warning of the crashes which are on the way. This tired little company is one of many in which a spot of timely margin analysis could have stimulated some early remedial action.*

This is not being wise after the event; I had pointed these trends out to the group during my earlier time there, but they were not inclined to pay any attention. Their mantra was "Don't change anything; we like it the way it is".

16. MODULAR HORSES

A very active recruiter puts me in touch with a managing director whose financial controller, who is his brother, is off work with an illness which may take some months to clear. The business makes modular buildings, the sections being constructed in the factory and assembled rapidly on-site. A filling station takes about two days on site to complete, including connexions to power, water, electricity and sewage, and a two-storey motel takes about two weeks. The ebullient managing director, who is the major shareholder, arranges to meet me in his local bar at lunchtime on a quiet weekday.

He describes his business to me, talking at a level just loud enough for everyone in the pub to hear what he's saying. He's clearly used to being the big wheel locally. When I ask him about competitors he mentions a larger business about 20 miles away, and says "But we're smarter than they are; we can do the same buildings for 10% less than they do."

I've only just met him and already it's all-or-nothing.

"Let me get this straight," I reply, "They can get 11.1% more than you for doing exactly the same thing... and who did you say was smarter?"

You could hear the proverbial pin drop.

"Well, we can talk about that at the office," he replies, flustered. "Let's go and get started."

It is clear that: (a) he runs a good business, but (b) he focuses too much on sales instead of margins, and (c) he is neither as clever nor as all-powerful as he thinks he is. He's not alone; it's a widespread disease.

The finance department is run by the wife of one of the directors and she is clearly struggling, but equally clearly capable of doing the job with a little advice and support. When I point out that the finance office is too cramped and the lack of space is clearly impeding people's work, she says that there is no other office available. I point out that if she swaps offices with the one next to mine, she will have plenty of room and the entire finance team will be together. She mentions permission and I tell her "You've just got it".

In some jobs you go in softly, softly, and in others you do the opposite. With a managing director used to being dictatorial, it's an easy choice. He reacts visibly to my reorganising the offices, but doesn't say anything. I start the habit of joining the finance team when they have a coffee break in the morning, and we begin to get a dialogue going. It turns out that the monthly results aren't finalised until the middle of the following month, or even later if the managing director is away. I ask for a list of all the factors that prevent them from producing the accounts rapidly and accurately, and eventually when I get the list it isn't too long, and most of the barriers centre around the boss.

I prepare a list of the information I need from the boss each month, and when I present it to him I tell him I need it on the second day of each month.

"Why?" he asks.

"So we can complete and present the results rapidly" I reply, deadpan.

"But I already know what the result is."

"OK, what's the result for this last month?"

"Umm, well it's between [guess no 1] and [guess no 2]".

"Fine, but please let me have that info as soon as possible."

When it arrives eventually after more prompting, the result is nowhere near the range he has given me.

"There must be something wrong with your accounts" he says.

"They're not my accounts, they're yours" I reply, and I show him a couple of costs he has completely forgotten.

After a couple of such knockabout months he falls more or less into line, and I can start doing more useful things, such as going out with him to slow-paying customers and lubricating the debt collection process. He and some associates have a few high-quality flat race horses and he is occasionally on his car-phone to his colleagues. One day I hear him say "I don't want Pat Eddery on him, I want Jason Weaver. Pat's the best jockey in the world, but Jason has a great pair of hands for a novice horse."

Many years later I'm a guest of a recruitment company at a big race meeting at Doncaster and not having won anything all day I turn to the last race, which is a large collection of novice horses over a surprisingly long distance. A complete lottery, in fact... but I remember that conversation in the car, and search for Weaver's name. He is riding, so I put a large amount of money on his unheard-of mount at very long odds. Everyone else in the hospitality suite is glued to the TV screen, but I'm sitting over at the bar with my good friend Jack Daniel, paying no attention and trying to appear super-cool (actually, I'm too scared to look).

Out of nowhere, Weaver and his mount come dancing through the mêlée to win by a couple of lengths, and to this day I'm up overall on horse racing, despite many losses, thanks to that one big bet at very long odds. Everyone in the party demands to know how I "knew" that horse was going to win, but I just smile, shrug my shoulders and order another Jack's.

To get back to the subject... the financial director returns after about three months and I can hand the reins back to him in reasonable shape, give or take a few remaining rough edges. I urge him not to back down when arguing with his dominating (perhaps I should say domineering) brother now that the finance department is in a position of relative strength, but I'm reasonably sure that it will prove difficult. It's one thing to be hard with a stranger, but more difficult with close kin.

Eventually he does move away. Family ties are seldom a good basis for business. Moreover, the work he and I have done to provide the company with a rapidly produced, informative and instructive monthly information pack is wasted on his brother, who still thinks he knows it all already.

LESSONS

A. *When dealing with a blusterer, bring him gently but firmly down to size as early as possible. Show him, preferably by some simple action,* *that you are unimpressed by his bluster. If he takes offence and gets rid of you, you're better off without him anyway.*

B. *Do not tolerate late monthly accounting. In this era there are very few businesses which are genuinely unable to produce rapid monthly reports.*

C. *The three Rs... not only RAPID, the reports should be RELIABLE and RELEVANT. This means that you may have to change parts of the format several times in a financial year to ensure that the main issues are brought to the attention of the business heads. Changes were needed here.*

17. SNACK ATTACK

This is a really odd one. A company making snacks with a solid market share wants to do long-term projections (typically 5/6/7-year ones). The company is well established organisationally and part of a large group with a high reputation, and has all of the necessary resources, especially in personnel terms, to do its own forecasting to a sensible degree of credibility (even bearing in mind that the demand for consumer products can be fickle). They don't seem to need any outsiders, but I'm more than happy to be involved.

I construct a conventionally-linked model in which the percentages drive the monetary numbers, not the other way around. The managers can therefore review in detail the effect of the variables on the profit and cash flow. It's always important to test such models, if not to destruction then at least to the limits of feasibility, and since this is a relatively simple manufacturing-and-selling model, that doesn't take long. The only thing I'm missing is the modelling of the advertising campaigns, both in terms of the monetary input and the extent (presumably in percentage terms, but just possibly in monetary terms) to which the promotions will generate volume and net profit.

This is where it comes unstuck. The marketing director says "Umm... put one million in there, a half-million in that year, and half-millions in those two years. No, on second thoughts, make that one there a million."

"So what effects will these have on the revenue lines?" I ask, wondering how that should be modelled. The response is similarly macro rather than micro: "Umm, increase that product line by a million the year after, then half a million the next year. Then this lot can increase for half a million for each of the next three years... and better stick a half-million on those ones for year number 5."

"Do you want me to do the effects of percentage variations on volumes?" I wonder aloud.

"No-no, those numbers'll do fine, thanks."

I persist: "And have you got outline plans for your advertising campaigns?"

"No-no, we do those nearer the time. We haven't thought them up yet."

Not the hard-nosed, intricately calculated campaign I was expecting... inevitably I'm more than a little sceptical about this approach. After a discussion with the managing director, however, I am reassured. The MD tells me that they know fairly accurately from long experience how big an advertising budget is needed to launch a new stream of products or boost an existing stream, and what effect half a million pounds of publicity will have on the top line. Their margins are generally consistent as they price their products on a cost-plus basis and the quality of their products remains high.

They thank me for my input and for building the model, and I take my leave armed with a large box of their products which they have kindly given me. As I type this, I have just checked their range of products on the internet, and they appear to be doing as well as ever. Most impressive.

I must admit that I don't know how they do it... I wasn't there long enough.

LESSONS

There are times when you consider that the work you have done is inadequate, but the client insists that you've done what he asks. This could mean one of two things:

A. *The client is not entirely happy with what you have done, and is looking for a non-contentious way of ending the project.*

B. *The client genuinely considers that what you have done meets their requirements, however unsatisfactory the outcome may appear to you.*

I got the impression that it was outcome B, but I cannot prove it!

18. PUBLIC TO PRIVATE (OR THE REVERSE)

The strange title isn't my fault. This is about reorganising a division of a public sector body in the UK in order to float it separately on the London Stock Exchange. In other words, a business which is intensely private in the public sector is going to become intensely public in the private sector... who dreamt up this terminology?

Introduction to the Managing Director: he is quiet, crisp, clear and concise, the kind of person who doesn't make a lot of waves but knows exactly where he is headed and how to get there. It is clear from his choice of words that he is an authoritarian, but a quiet one who eschews histrionics; in fact, ideal. My given objectives are to turn his team of public sector functional managers into a team of private sector business managers, and to handle any related issues which crop up along the way. Of those there are plenty.

Task number one is therefore to get hold of some numbers by which the team can be guided and measured. This is a large public sector body and they have 1,600 accounting codes for our division: not only is there a separate code for the cost of cleaning windows, but there are separate window-cleaning codes for each department... I therefore know exactly what it costs to clean secretaries' windows and personnel department windows, etc., but it doesn't do me (nor anyone else) any good. Task number one therefore defines itself. It takes a week to remove a zero from the number of codes, but the process turns out to be a very effective way of getting to know the structure of the business, and we have it summarised in around 160 codes.

OK, we have some numbers. What next? We have to start using them to control the division as a separate business, so a budget is worked out with the MD and managers, aligned with a set of target dates for the various stages in transforming the department into a stand-alone business.

A major distraction is a team of consultants originally brought in by the public sector body for several purposes. Although these consultants are intelligent and hard-working, they are not taking us any nearer our goal, which is to be a profitable stand-alone business. Moreover, their fees are making a big hole in the financial performance. After some discussion and some gentle politicking, the local authority is persuaded to part with them.

Another problem is the introduction of a "chief executive" who is wildly expensive and whose aims we consider to be beyond the bounds of realism. He comes across as a megalomaniac villain in a James Bond movie; all that is missing is a white cat for him to stroke while he speaks.

For instance, when we discuss with him the SWOT analysis for inclusion in the strategic plan he insists on transferring one or two items which we have identified as weaknesses into the strengths category. We refuse point-blank to follow his instructions; our rationale is that although the resources in question are effective, they are not as effective as those of many of our competitors; they are therefore weaknesses, not strengths. Fortunately we are able to part with the chief executive before long in relation to a technical matter, and continue with our existing and much more capable MD.

As if we didn't have enough on our plates, there is a move to new premises to accelerate our status as an entity entirely separate from the local authority. Added to the other changes already in process, this places considerable strain on the staff, and complaints multiply. We hold a meeting to discuss the necessity to get the staff fully on board with us.

"We're not communicating enough" say the management team.

"No," I argue, "We're communicating too much. Through no fault of our own, some of the things we say we'll do don't happen as planned, and people get justifiably disgruntled. From now on we don't promise anything; we just do it. In the meantime, we need a few quick hits to improve their lot, starting with a much better coffee machine, a cold drinks machine, a snack machine, a dedicated smokers' room, a jokey little monthly company news sheet with puzzles and prizes and so on. Don't do it all at once; just keep up the little improvements a few days apart until they realise that things are very much on the upward path.

And whatever you do, don't announce these things."

It works. The staff, who are a sensible bunch, begin to notice the improvements and settle down, and before long we hear the welcome sound of cheerful banter in the main office.

There follows the detailed process of moving from a public sector department to a public limited company; it doesn't distract the customer-facing staff very much, and the local authority gives us help in setting up separate systems. We now have our own lively systems support team and our stand-alone systems are fully functional and securely backed up. We shed rapidly the remaining paraphernalia of a local authority and become fully commercial.

What we need next is performance. The fact that the organisational issues have largely been resolved means that we can focus on profit and cash flow, aided by some specific financial training for the related staff, and we are now a bona fide commercial outfit. When the budget is launched, we do not let it die, as often happens. The sales force in particular are held nose-to-the-grindstone on this, and they respond handsomely with some very worthwhile new business. Every month begins with a meeting on how we will beat our net margin (as opposed to sales) targets for the following month, the current month having already been targeted.

I run a number of in-house courses to channel our already-solid admin and finance teams into customer-facing units, very much focused on the outside world. Inevitably a number of hiccups occur in the transition from public-sector structural thinking to private-sector commercial thinking, but overall the response is an almost-tangible surge in performance and therefore morale. People like making money.

Behind all this is a managing director who combines relentless pressure with highly visible recognition of good performance. When someone does things well, everyone gets to know about it. And we know when we've done well because we're measuring all aspects of our performance, and those measurements are transmitted to and understood by the staff.

Suddenly, I'm superfluous. The outfit is fully operational, without needing any external help. It's a buoyant feeling for all of us.

A little project in California beckons. Or maybe not such a little project.

Immediately.

How immediately?

"BA exec lounge, London Heath Row, half-past eight tomorrow morning."

Click.

LESSONS

A. *A public sector body generally works to a cost budget rather than an income budget, but this one, for historical reasons, had a commercial activity which could operate quite independently if organised to do so. Floating the commercial activity would leave the local authority to concentrate on its normal activities in looking after the needs of the population in its area. This meant that the training of the management team had to involve creating an entirely new culture – a culture of profit instead of one of cost.*

B. *The accounting and systems issues were very conventional and their adaptation required practical work rather than intellectual development.*

C. *The stand-alone operation which was being floated needed to be groomed to be customer-oriented to the point of seeking a profit on all of its activities, and meeting every single monthly budget target in the process. This involved pointing the sales team very firmly towards gaining new business, but fortunately they were already well down that road, and full of enthusiasm. Once they appreciated the numbers by which they were measured, they took great pride in beating those numbers as often and by as big a margin as they could.*

Previously any sales of facilities were to some extent regarded by the local authority as a reduction of the cost of those facilities, but the sales were now the raison d'être of the spun-out business. It was therefore necessary from the beginning of the change-over to create a constant pressure on the sales force to obtain new business at suitably profitable margins every single month.

D. *If any one contract fell through or was postponed, there had to be an immediate hunt for replacement business, sometimes by bringing a future contract forward. This involved close liaison by the sales force with the technical planners and operatives who provided and installed the products.*

E. *You don't need superstars; you just need sensible, committed people who will work hard as a team.*

F. *Note: SWOT stands for "Strengths, Weaknesses, Opportunities, Threats", a simple and effective way of depicting a business's status in its market.*

19. SAN ANDREAS AND OTHER FAULTS

I drive through the evening straight from the previous project to Newcastle (the one upon the Tyne, with the accent on the "castle") and return my hired car to its owners, then head for the airport, where I'll sleep overnight and catch the early flight to London Heathrow. Usually in such circumstances I sleep along three or four adjacent seats, but these seats are all bucket seats, so I have to sleep underneath them instead, alongside my kitbag. Not comfortable, but I manage to be in passable shape for the flight to LHR.

There I meet the Chairman, whom I had met previously in the course of the very short project number 11, and we board a flight for Los Angeles. Sleep, blissful sleep, occasionally interrupted by the Chairman throwing peanuts at me from across the aisle. We arrive at LAX (the code and nickname for LA's airport) ahead of schedule and board a domestic flight for San Diego, where we meet the group's engineering director, who is based in Placentia, on the outskirts of Los Angeles, but is down at San Diego for our meeting.

After checking in at our hotel in San Diego, we go straight into a meeting. The background is as follows:

The Chairman heads a group of light engineering companies of medium to high technology. The group has lent the San Diego company a large amount of money to complete the development of some clever aerospace maintenance software which will be of great value to the military operators especially. The loan terms specify that San Diego are only to provide aircraft manufacturers with the "vanilla" version of the software, so that when the manufacturers inevitably wish to have it customised to their own precise needs, the company will gain considerable additional high-margin work.

Instead, the San Diego man (as of now, the ex-president) has disobeyed the terms of the arrangement and promised individually customised software to several aerospace companies, and as a result of these over-commitments the San Diego company has run out of funds and is unable to continue. But the conditions of the loan from UK specify that if there is catastrophic performance by the San Diego company, the UK company can convert its loan into capital, thereby gaining control of the company. That is exactly what is now happening.

The meeting is acerbic in the extreme and both the ex-president and his lawyer indulge in belligerent grandstanding, but the chairman holds the reins and does not budge an inch. He doesn't trust California lawyers, so we have a six-foot-plus Arizona lawyer with us, black-suited and black-haired, straight from the OK Corral in appearance. We are taking over the company with immediate effect, and it is arranged that I will go out to the company the next day to assess the situation.

The Chairman and Wyatt Earp are heading back to Los Angeles, where we are setting up a replacement office. The engineering director of the company, a comparatively sensible person, will become the new president when he returns to the LA area from his truncated golfing holiday in Hawaii.

Sleep, blissful sleep. I awake early.

Swimming is a linear activity, but for some reason architects who design hotels make the pools short and wide instead of long and narrow, so that you spend most of your time doing turns instead of actually swimming. But this open-air pool is different; beautifully landscaped around some rocks, it's at least 40 metres long and devoid of people at this early hour. Just beyond it is San Diego harbour, bordered by Coronado and the Pacific. Wonderful! After about 40 lengths of steady crawl the tiredness of travel has gone, and I decide not to be weighed down by breakfast.

Barefoot with a towel around my waist on the 23rd floor, I enter my room just as the Chairman is leaving his room next door. He calls my name and I step back into the corridor, only to hear the click of my door shutting on its spring, with my key inside. Out of devilment the Chairman has a ten-minute conversation with me while I'm wearing nothing but a towel, before he heads down to the dining room and sends up a porter with a master-key to rescue me.

The first stop is at the company's accounting firm. The taxi driver has very little English and eventually I ascertain that he is from

Somalia, so I can communicate with him in a few halting words of long-forgotten Swahili. The company accountant has already been briefed by telephone from UK, so we quickly reach an agreement by which I can access his records, such as they are, when I need them. Then it's off to the company office, this time driven by an Afghan taxi driver who claims he flew MiG jets for the Soviet air force. Given the way he drives, I'm tempted to believe him. I communicate with him in broken Russian vaguely remembered from the Ukraine and Siberia projects, and we get somehow to the company office, out in the desert.

The company is housed in what is clearly meant to be a dwelling house, built on a steep slope. The upper storey opens into the slope and the lower storey, of a much smaller footprint, faces outward and downward. The ex-president's wife, huge, surly and track-suited, is drinking Pepsi through a straw from a large waxed cardboard bucket bearing the inscription "Gulp Me" in big letters, and meets me sourly on the upper floor. I tell her I need to see the financial records, and having already been briefed by her aggressive husband, she has had them laid out on the board-room table for me.

I should mention that the company has a branch office in Canada, near Ottawa. This may be a little hard to believe, but she has recorded the Canadian transactions in Canadian dollars in the same ledger accounts that she has used for the US transactions in US dollars. The totals of the accounts are therefore meaningless. Is this a world first? Possibly. I ply her with sharp questions until she becomes rattled, claims to have a meeting elsewhere and departs in a hurry, which is exactly what I want.

Quickly I gather up the accounting records, head round to the basement door facing down the slope and introduce myself to the software engineer, who has been briefed by the chairman and is on our side. Also downstairs is the similarly voluminous son of the ex-president and his wife, ostensibly designing software with his sneaker-clad feet on the desk and a ghetto-blaster belting out a strange mixture of rap and rock. His sweat-shirt tells me he is a San Diego Padres fan. We all have our crosses to bear.

As I examine the records in the next room, the engineer disappears in his pick-up truck and returns towing a U-Haul trailer (which you can hire at any of their US depots and return to any of their other depots, an excellent arrangement).

While junior continues to plot world domination to the sound of his oversized tranny, the software engineer and I strip out the filing cabinets and load the trailer with all of the records. By late afternoon we have emptied the place thoroughly, and without even notifying junior we head off for the freeway north to Los Angeles. Darkness is falling and we hear police sirens. My heart leaps and my blood seems to run cold, but they're not after us. We aren't breaking any laws, being under orders from the company's legal officials, but it would take a considerable amount of explaining to a couple of local cops if the San Diego crew called to complain.

As we head up the coastal freeway in darkness an ear-splitting roar shatters the night.

"F-15" says the software engineer.

"Surely an F-14?" I query, having seen Top Gun.

"F-15, definitely" he says, "Only an F-15 can make that much noise".

(Years later, an F-15E circles very low over our hilltop house in the Scottish Borders, and I now believe him).

Somewhere along the coast the engineer pulls off the freeway and heads down a small road, ending up at a neat little flat-roofed bungalow on the shore. This is his pad, where we will spend the night. One wall of the lounge is taken up with a large tank full of tropical fish swimming lazily and in the opposite wall is one long window. Outside this giant picture window is a paved barbecue area, bordered by a low wall beyond which some good-sized Pacific breakers are curling in under the moonlight. Indoors a couple of surfboards are suspended from the lounge ceiling.

Either I'm starring in a movie or I've died and this is paradise. The engineer rustles up a couple of tasty steaks to complete the illusion.

Somewhere in the evening's conversation he mentions that he is extremely annoyed with his sister. When I ask why, he growls that she was engaged once upon a time to a young software developer called Bill Gates, but she broke off the engagement.

The next morning we head for the other office of the company, near Placentia, inland some miles from Los Angeles. The office is on the upper floor of a hacienda-style building designed around four sides of a garden with a fish pond and fountain. Near the fountain some kids are acting suspiciously, probably dealing drugs. This is where our sensible managing director works, or will do when he returns from his Hawaiian holiday as the new president.

"Wait here" says the software man and disappears, returning soon with three Mexicans. "Five dollars an hour plus all the Coke they can drink" he explains, as they unload the trailer and stack the records in the office. I pay off the cheerful Mexicans and he attends to setting up his software office while I do my best to stack the boxes of records in some kind of reasonable order. It's a Saturday and I'm glad to get some rest in a nearby hotel.

Useless information: in the era of this escapade, Pepsi out-sells Coke across the USA, except in California, where the numerous Mexican population drinks Coke. Recently, however, Coke appears to be overhauling Pepsi in the USA, leaving Scotland (where Irn Bru allegedly reigns supreme) and the Islamic countries as the only non-communist parts of the world in which Coke is not the highest-selling soft drink.

After two days spent sorting the records as logically as possible, we are glad to see the president (vice-president until a few days ago) and his manager returning from their golfing holiday in Hawaii. We haven't recalled them previously because it was easier to deal with the ex-president on his own, and we now have two reasonably sensible, orderly and capable people to run the business. The software engineer is already back to work, and two other technical people arrive, so that we are once again producing logistics software for aviation and military purposes, which is what we are here for.

But that is not all. We still have an embittered and uncontrollable ex-president and his wife down near San Diego, capable of putting a spanner in the works. We also need a new accounting system and somebody to run it, and interviews are scheduled for an administrator. A tall, very smart, flame-haired Irish-American woman with a Mexican name and a lime-green suit leaves the other interviewees far behind in the opinion of the managers, and we email a sample of her handwriting to one of the group managers in the UK. The sample comprises only a signature on a photocopy of a fax of a photocopy (email is only just starting to take over) but he faxes back to us what turns out to be a remarkably accurate psycho-analysis of the woman. No way is he ever going to get my signature.

She starts immediately and within days has the office running like clockwork, even setting up the board meetings properly and taking excellent minutes. Sometimes you get lucky. The software wizard gives us a schedule of estimated project completion dates and at last we have a business under way and under some kind of control.

On her desk the administrator has a photo of two girls with a vaguely familiar-looking gent. Who's that? Oh, that's me and my sister with Mel Gibson. Ask a stupid question; this is California, dammit.

We even have some money; a cheque for $130,000 from one of the aerospace companies is received and banked down at San Diego. A cheque for that amount is sent from the ex-president at San Diego, signed by him and his wife, to us in Placentia. He has to behave, or he won't get his compensation money. But then his solicitor instructs him to recall the cheque, and he invokes a little-known banking rule of the company that a cheque may not be signed by two related persons, so that the cheque is frozen by the bank instead of being cleared. The bank manager was not aware of this rule, but on checking the terms of the account, he agrees that the cheque must be frozen, despite the fact that they have been breaking that rule for years.

Without the cheque we are almost cashless. The UK office gets some money to me by an emergency route, and I try to open an account at the local Wells Fargo, who clearly think it is hot money or some kind of scam, and I get nowhere. However, the president opens up a bank account for the company with just one quick phone-call. It's a quirk of the USA that people are suspicious of cash in any form, but not of credit.

The $130,000 remains frozen, but I have a plan for that, and we leave it for the time being. The organisation is now operational, and negotiations to buy out the other director are being settled from UK at $500,000. I ask the managing director to agree a payment of $250,000 up front, followed by $125,000 and $125,000 at 3-monthly intervals, provided that the other director behaves himself. More about that later.

It is the late 1990s and email is rapidly becoming the standard method of transmission of data. We are about to email technical software to various internationally-known companies in the USA when someone asks me "Does that count as an in-state sale or an out-of-state sale?"

Good question. Out-of-state sales are not taxable, but in-state sales bear sales tax. I phone the technical department of our auditors, and of one other Big Four accounting firm, and ask for a paper on the subject to be submitted to us within 24 hours, at an agreed price. The next day the papers duly arrive; one says it's an in-state sale and therefore taxable, while the other states that it's an out-of-state sale and therefore tax-free. I leave it up to the president to choose how he wants to deal with it, bearing in mind that there will be many such sales!

There is a useful accountant operating in a mall across the six-lane highway from the office, and I engage him to provide us with a monthly financial statement and help us with tax and other services, superseding the San Diego accountant. I also note that the software engineer takes the software back-ups home to his surfer pad down the coast every night, and I change this arrangement to storing the back-ups in a fire-proof safe in the accountant's office. When the president hears of this, he goes ballistic. Why?

"Earthquake!" he rants at me. The accountant's office is several hundred yards away, and safe from a fire in the office, but the software engineer's surfer pad down the coast is beyond the San Andreas Fault, which is a much greater concern. I live and learn.

We are up and running, and our new administrator is even correcting the grammar in the Chairman's minutes, much to his delight. Christmas is looming, and ever since Thanksgiving it's been wall-to-wall Jingle Bells, so it's time to go. Negotiations to buy out the El Cajon team are being processed by the President and I'm not needed any more. Time for the great silver bird, although the project isn't quite dead yet. Read on.

Several months later, when I'm working for the same group in Ohio... .

There is still that little matter of the cheque for $130,000 which was frozen by the outgoing San Diego manager on the grounds that cheques were not allowed to be signed by two related persons. I have arranged with the President that the buy-out from the San Diego man will be split into three instalments, the last of which will be $125,000. When the time comes for payment of the final instalment, the Chairman tells the San Diego director to contact me at my next project, in Cleveland.

He comes on the phone, belligerently: "Where's my 125,000 dollars?"

"You've got it already"

"No, we have not. I want it now."

"Remember that cheque for $130,000 that you had frozen back in November?"

"Yep. So what?"

"Well, it's all yours now, with my compliments."

He goes through all of the swearwords in Webster's and a few Spanish ones to boot.

"Have a really nice day" I reply, and hang up.

If the final payment had been $130,000 he'd have smelt a rat, which was why we chose the instalment of £125,000. The chairman and I agreed that it would be worth the extra $5,000 to have him go to the bank to eat humble pie and confess to having been seriously obstructive. Whether the original cheque is still valid or he has to wheedle another one from the aerospace client I don't know, but it's a sweet, sweet moment.

There's no justice like poetic justice.

LESSONS

A. *California is mad, but the madness can be good fun.*

B. *You're nobody in the USA if you don't have a credit card. Or several.*

C. *The internal revenue service doesn't appear to have the same* *control over companies and regulations as exists in most European countries.*

D. *Development of software must be VERY strictly controlled, as it will otherwise easily and rapidly get out of hand.*

E. *Outsiders don't trust California lawyers. In fact, even Californians don't trust them to any great extent. That's why many Arizona lawyers also qualify in California law and make a good living from it.*

F. *The software which operates the North American airliner in which you may be flying as you read this was probably designed by a lunatic.*

20. BANKS OF THE CUYAHOGA

The group for whom I've been working in sunny California (come to think of it, it hadn't been that sunny; El Niño had been making its presence felt and the weather had been unusually patchy; almost British, in fact) have a project for me on the outskirts of Cleveland. The Cuyahoga river used to be so polluted that it once caught fire, but Cleveland has cleaned it up till it sparkles in the winter sun (as does the whole city). The UK client wants me to have an initial meeting with them before I go home for Christmas.

The tannoy at Cleveland airport instructs Mr Drysdale from Los Angeles to meet Mrs Drysdale at a certain point, and I'm racking my brains to figure out what my wife is doing here. But it turns out that the owner-manager's name is Drysdale and it is his wife who greets me, takes me to dinner, tells me a lot about the company and deposits me at a motel a short distance from the factory.

The boss, who has been away white-water rafting through the Grand Canyon, arrives in a couple of days and is more interested in trying to find whether we have common ancestry than in giving me an induction into the company. He is genuinely appalled that I know almost nothing of my ancestry and have never tried to research it, and I have to explain to him that as my birth certificate states that I was born in Scotland I don't have to prove that my forebears come from that country. Anyway, I was raised in East Africa and my passport states that I'm British, so I'm not strongly one nationality or another.

I'm given a useful intro to the company and its workings. It makes emission control equipment for a variety of industrial sites around and beyond the USA, and is a good mixture of basic metal-bashing and sophisticated electronics. The accounting software is a nightmare, as is the suite of management accounting schedules sent by the group controller in the UK, but these things can be fixed. The factory itself is well-organised and kept immaculate. Time for a holiday back home over Christmas, and for trying to remember not to speak to my wife in the North American accent I've acquired.

In January I return via Reykjavík, a route that includes a free night in town and a tour of Reykjanes en route to the airport. The guide tells the bus passengers that Reykjavík means "smoky bay" and Reykjanes means "smoky headland" and is intrigued when I tell him that the terms "reekie wick" and "reeky ness" in Scotland have the same meanings. We then have a long argument as to who found whom in their longboats. The onward flight includes a long, slow descent over the New England coast, giving magnificent views, and after a change of plane at New York, I'm back in Cleveland.

The main part of the role is to get Cleveland reporting in the right format to London, and doing it on time, which necessitates much sharper information-gathering than is already in place. The performance reports are monthly, but the cash reports and forecasts are required weekly, which is fun, as the directors have never prepared weekly cash forecasts in their lives. Moreover, I have to do a lot of reasoning and exhorting to explain why the forecasts are needed weekly rather than monthly.

As the owner-manager is on the path to retirement when he sells the company to my client, there is also the question of finding a successor, and one becomes available from elsewhere in the client's group. This is a relief, as we now have a managing director on board who fully understands the need to provide three Rs (rapid, reliable, relevant) information regularly to the group HQ. Moreover, the local directors do not hold regular meetings and are not always in tune with each other, so the advent of a head honcho to take over from the owner and run the business on a more systematic basis is a big step forward. Gradually the path is smoothed out (reluctantly in the case of the sales director) and we become noticeably more professional.

A huge fall of snow brings the whole of the Cleveland area to a halt. There are three categories of snow, but this is so severe that they give it a special category four (Manila all over again). Until further notice, anyone who drives without police permission will be arrested. When the roads are cleared, which happens astonishingly quickly (the USA are unparalleled when it comes to doing physical things on a large scale), life returns to normal in Cleveland and the outlying area.

Around this time, I realise with horror that my stay in the USA has only two more days to run. I try to get an extension, but to no avail.

While looking for the passport office downtown, I ask someone in the foyer of a skyscraper if I'm in the right building. He tells me that it's the next building, then asks me if I'm from England. I tell him "No, Scotland" and he recoils, says "Oh, I know all about that; I've seen the movie" and half-runs out of the building.

Thank you, Mel Gibson... next time I'm over here, I'll paint my face blue and scare everyone, not just the occasional passer-by.

The flights to Toronto and Ottawa pass without event, but the drive from Ottawa to our office at Kanata reveals the enormous devastation caused by the recent ice storm. Entire forests of colossal fir trees have been brought to the ground under the weight of the ice accumulated on them in the recent storms. I spend a day at Kanata checking out the Canadian office, which is well ordered, and then it's back to Ottawa and then Toronto. The clerk at the check-in for Cleveland takes one look at my passport, with its two entries to USA already expired, and hustles me through to a back room, which is occupied by... the CIA. Fortunately, my flight is two hours away.

The guy behind the desk is a seasoned pro. He takes me question-by-question through my entire life, frequently backtracking to see if I give a different answer to my previous one, and I'm fascinated by the process; the guy is the real deal. Eventually he appears to relax, and says "OK, let's get your form filled in for Uncle Sam" and talks out loud as he fills in the form. But even then, he deliberately mis-states the data for the form to try and catch me out, and I have to correct him.

When he hands back my passport with the visa extension completed, I say "I've been done over by the KGB; you'll be glad to know that you're a whole lot more professional than they are. But I have a question. There are 40 US jobs riding on this project, and yet I'm having a hard time getting back into the country, but in the time we've been talking, probably a dozen illegals have slipped into the USA by some other route. How do you feel about that?"

He scowls and shakes his head slowly. "Don't go there" he growls.

Clearly a sore point.

Occasionally during the Cleveland stint I have to go back to Los Angeles, and on one trip the Kanata manager and I meet at LA airport wrapped up for a northern winter, to find ourselves in what feels like summer. We remove coats, scarves, boots, etc., for the long taxi ride, but we muffle up again with only our eyes showing for our dramatic entry into the shirt-sleeved boardroom, and receive a standing ovation, followed by an ice-cold Pepsi.

On another occasion I've just flown in from Cleveland when the snow is so bad up there that they've declared another special category 4 (more shades of Manila). But even at this time of night (0300) LA is decidedly warm, and I'm ridiculously and uncomfortably over-dressed. There are dozens of cars around and hundreds of people, but no taxis, and the situation does not look promising.

Suddenly an enormous white stretch-limo with darkened windows pulls in effortlessly from the chaos and halts in front of me. One window slides down. The driver, an immaculately dressed gent who looks like a much larger version of Barry White, purrs "You goin' someplace?"

"Placentia," I reply, shedding some of my Nanook-of-the-North garments.

We agree 40 bucks and I slide into the back.

"You like music?" asks the big guy. "I'm a piano man."

I think that means that I ought to be a piano man, too.

"George Shearing? Oscar Peterson?" I suggest, trying to sound casual, as if I would actually know either of them from Ramsey Lewis, or for that matter, Jerry Lee Lewis.

"Man, you talkin' my language," he murmurs, and the big limo pulls effortlessly out of LAX on to the I-105, heading for Placentia to the sound of rippling ivories.

I'm half listening to the music, half trying to recognise points on the route, to work out whether we really are going to Placentia or whether I've ended up in some movie or other by mistake. But he takes me straight to my motel, and I give him an extra 10 bucks for such a smooth journey. He probably owns a luxury pad up in Canyonlands by now.

That's quite enough about California. Back to Ohio.

The business at Cleveland needs a financial controller to take over from me on a permanent basis. I'm given a budget from HQ and am recommended to use a local recruiter who has a high reputation, justified as it turns out. She provides a long list of candidates; we whittle it down to 10 and start interviewing. The result is awful;

although quite bright, they are all robotic, saying what they think are the right things to say and not showing the slightest spark of individuality. They are also excruciatingly politically correct, which isn't much use, especially if they have to deal with Brits. I manage to select two, one of each sex, fortunately, although I'm not very optimistic. The group financial director comes over for their second interviews, and not surprisingly he blows them out.

I tell him that we need to offer a much higher salary to get the right person, and we increase the salary on offer by about 60%. The first of the new candidates enters and we get settled. He interrupts my first post-introduction statement with "I don't agree with that" and then tells me precisely why, and I spend the rest of the interview not really listening to him, but thinking carefully how I am going to hook him. It goes well, and he makes his mark with the Group FD when he comes over from the UK again for the second interview. We have our finance director, and he's not a shrinking violet.

I work in parallel with him for a short period, and then it's time to leave him on his own. He has struck up a positive partnership with the new managing director and suddenly three's a crowd. My wife arrives from the UK, without any luggage as instructed, and we spend a few hours in a Cleveland department store buying all the practical clothes we could wish for, at fraction of the price they would be in the UK (and generally better made).

She would like to see two things: the Grand Canyon and Yellowstone, which are far to the south and far to the north respectively. No sweat: we fly to Salt Lake City, pick up our reserved camper van and spend two perfect weeks exploring the Great Divide from Arizona to Wyoming. It is early May and most of the tourist spots have opened for business, but the holiday season has not begun and we appear to have the whole of the western states all to ourselves. Magnifico.

While we're away I phone my successor a couple of times, but he has no problems; the guy is a consummate operator and it's time to leave him in charge. He and the managing director work well together and go on to many successes in later life. After a final couple of days back at Cleveland ensuring that my closets are skeleton-free, I head back to the UK with my wife.

LESSONS

A. *North Americans are generally technically excellent in business, but their day-to-day management of the details and procedures leaves a lot to be desired. The more scientific they are in their métier, the worse they are at the basics of running a business. To some extent this is to be expected; someone who is wrapped up in some new technological development is hardly likely to be interested in the calculation of the amortisation of the fixed assets for the current month. Moreover, dealing with technical objects is very different from dealing with people, something they tend to forget.*

B. *The quality of professional advice for small companies is well below that generally found in Western Europe. I'll make an exception for some of the lawyers, though; Wyatt Earp is very sharp and our lady in Cleveland is from the same no-nonsense mould.*

C. *US tax systems can be somewhat oblique. No, make that "very oblique". Get help.*

21. CELTIC CONNEXION

I've been lucky enough to visit every county in England, even Rutland; they are varied and characterful, and I enjoy trying to imitate the local accents, some more successfully than others. The most beautiful (and most musical) of them all is the one I can see a few miles away from where I'm typing this: Northumberland, a quiet stretch of varied landscapes, castles, islands, beautiful coastline and an air of timeless Celtic mystery. Cue a thousand clichés; you still won't do it justice.

Unfortunately the small company I go to see isn't in the same serene state as the county in which it is situated. The company makes software specifically designed for libraries and it has had great potential until... the nature of the "until" is what I have to determine. A group of business angels have invested a sizeable amount of money under a well-conceived government scheme but are now being urgently asked to put in some more. What has gone adrift?

It's a long story, but the gist of it is this: a very clever and capable software package has been developed for use for libraries, giving them a range of day-to-day management advantages hitherto unavailable. The first thing I learn is that instead of making a standard "vanilla" package for sale and then earning additional revenue by offering and selling add-on facilities when they have been fully developed and tested, the managing director has over-committed the company to its customers and potential customers, promising to each one all manner of customised facilities from the outset. San Diego rides again.

Shared code is in use, causing customisation of one customer's software to create problems in other customers' software. As small companies can easily do when a market opens up, this business has over-committed itself and is in serious trouble.

Choosing me to do this job is maybe not the best idea, as although I use computers extensively I know little about their inner workings. However, the first main technical requirement is to standardise the working procedures themselves so that each individual project in progress is isolated from changes to other projects. The second, concurrent with the first, is to get some money in, which means concentrating on the most advanced projects and finishing them to get them out to customers and collect the cash.

Easier said than done. The managing director is one of those infuriating clients who always has to be somewhere else, no matter what commitments he has to cancel, and is thus almost impossible to pin down. My initial interview with him is a straggly session of diversions and irrelevances, and it tells me nothing other than to be very wary.

Next stop the finance department, consisting of three young people who are clearly competent and able to hold their own against any manager making unreasonable demands on the finances. Nevertheless, the balance sheet is a bit ragged-looking, and we need to get cash in, so I ask for a list of customers whose software is near to completion.

Although the disasters stem from the (mis-)managing director, the technical manager is rock-solid and realistic, and I will need to spend some time with him. Meanwhile, I learn that the business angels away in the city are putting in another tranche of money, so I mentally cross my fingers that this supportive action will bear rewards.

The first thing you should do accounts-wise in investigating any business is to dig beyond the balance sheet... that's where the bad news is hidden... or the good news is invented. The receivables are proving difficult to collect, a fact that the finance team have already pointed out, so we may have some write-offs there. The inventory comprises mainly work-in-progress, in which there are a large number of project accounts, most of them with similar values. In fact, all of them have similar values.

Oh, no...

I don't believe it. On the instructions of the managing director, the value of the basic software has been debited to each customer account on the basis that the customer is committed to that project and the software already exists. So instead of the software being in the balance sheet as a single fixed asset, it is replicated throughout the receivables ledger without the work having been finished. The young members of the finance department confirm that that is what they have been explicitly told to do.

I learn that a local accountant comes in and prepares monthly financial statements from the ledgers, but he does not audit the figures nor provide a balance sheet because he is neither instructed to nor paid to. Fair enough.

So we have a grossly inflated balance sheet. The only avenue left is to go hell-for-leather to complete the most advanced projects and hand them over to the customers. We have an emergency meeting with the technical manager and the senior software personnel and agree a list of the projects which can be completed in the shortest time. These projects are to have absolute priority over all others. By this time the managing director has disappeared completely and nobody, not even his secretary, knows where he is.

The company is based in two buildings. The main office is in a smart and pleasant riverside building, specially fitted out by the town council for small businesses, and the software department of more than a dozen people is in a first-storey flat a few hundred yards away in the town centre. The technical manager drives the software team while the finance department and I try to find ways through the money barriers.

But it is all to no avail. I have to go to the business angels' office in the big city and tell them that the company is insolvent and therefore trading illegally. They immediately question the role of the local accountant, but I point out that he was not instructed (nor paid) to carry out any audit work. Back at the company I keep trying to find some possible avenue for funds, but really I'm just awaiting the inevitable.

When the liquidator's team arrive I call everyone together in the main office by the river and break the news. There is a near-riot, everybody demanding loudly to know where the managing director is. As soon as I can, I leave the office under control of the liquidation team and sprint for the software flat. As I open the street door I see the software staff coming down the stairs carrying PCs, printers and anything else they can take.

I shout up the stairs: "Don't be bloody stupid; the Police are outside! You'll get arrested and have a criminal record!"

Of course it isn't true; the police are nowhere, but the staff don't know that. I tell them they can help themselves to diskettes (remember them?), manuals and any small items, but computers and printers, all of them leased, must stay. Bit by bit the staff get sorted out. Eventually they realise that there are no policemen outside, but by that time the rage has subsided.

I tell them that I will help the team leaders to write their CVs up-to-date, and that the team leaders will then help the rest of the staff with their CVs. We get a system arranged for that, and addresses and phone numbers are swapped so that it can happen soon. Inevitably some residual anger occasionally flares up and I get locked into a side-office for a while, but someone releases me and I get back to the main office.

The liquidator's team have taken over, and I check that the finance team are not being hassled, but they have already adapted to the new circumstances and are helping the liquidator's team and the other members of staff. It's a long day and I don't get away until well into the evening, when everyone else has gone. I live an hour's drive away, so I take a note of the telephone numbers of the senior personnel and give them mine in case of any urgent issues. The liquidator's team are now in control of the two premises.

The next morning, a remarkable piece of news is received. The managing director's house has caught fire during the night and a big blaze ensues before the fire brigade can douse the flames. The CID start interviewing employees, but I call the police station and point out that the employees have no interest in destroying any assets; quite the opposite, in fact. Most people involved have come to a much more sinister conclusion. The managing director has disappeared, and a few days later is vaguely rumoured to have arrived in his mother's house via the bathroom window.

I get one of the admin staff to peruse the yellow pages in the phone directories of the neighbouring counties and list the names, numbers and addresses of all the software and related companies and circulate the list to all employees to help them find another job. A good number of them succeed remarkably quickly.

Some of the shareholders are looking for blood and consider an action against the accountant who prepared the monthly figures. I point out that, as was evidenced by his letter of engagement and the modest size of his fee, he was under no requirement whatsoever to perform any audit checks on the figures, nor had anyone instructed him or even asked him to do so. Eventually they drop the matter, very reluctantly.

Altogether, a sad case... I never get to hear what has happened to the managing director or his house, but I'm kindly invited to a couple of get-togethers of the former employees, who all appear to be in good form despite their recent tribulations. The business angels are very ethical and go to some trouble to find me my next project.

LESSONS

A. *Instructing a local accountant to prepare a monthly profit statement without including a reasonable level of review of the balance sheet is taking a big risk. The balance sheet is where the garbage is dumped and therefore should ALWAYS be reviewed.*

B. *These particular business angels were highly reputable, but did they do sufficient investigation into the fabric of the business before investing? Any kind of software is difficult for an outsider to evaluate in its development phase, so if the angels didn't have a software guru in their ranks, I'd have expected them to engage one to investigate the concept and its progress thoroughly before investing. This may have happened; I don't know.*

The MD could have shown them a perfectly good early demo before spinning it in many directions simultaneously. A tricky one!

C. *Walk before you can run. Self-evidently, if the company had started by selling the basic software and thereafter developed add-ons or special versions, it could have been a very successful enterprise. What an utter waste of talent and effort.*

22. SCANNERS & SPANNERS

I've heard of this company before. It designs, manufactures and sells high-resolution ultrasonic imaging equipment for medical and veterinary applications. The founders and directors were a married couple, but the husband died and his wife has determined bravely to continue the business as managing director. The company has technical staff who are capable of completing, producing and selling the designs of her husband, and one of the finance houses has provided a very intelligent, effective and empathetic non-executive director.

The situation with the managing director is thus:

- she is intelligent in many respects, but misguided in others
- she is running a veritable crusade for her late husband, and is determined to complete his work
- she is highly regarded in the medical ultrasonics world in her own right
- as far as possible she employs women rather than men
- she believes (with some justification) that women work better than men
- she especially employs women who have fallen on hard times
- she despises most men because in her opinion they don't match up to her late husband
- she has a low opinion of accountants and does not regard them as important (I'm used to that, but this is quite an extreme case)
- she knows that no purchase invoices have been processed for a few months, nor even properly authorised
- she does not consider that to be a priority
- her only finance/ accounting/ bookkeeping employee could use a lot of basic help, and perhaps a bit of practical advice here and there

Some of the above are understandable attitudes, but they are the kind of attitudes which can easily become disadvantageous.

Where to begin? Check out the management.

The technical manager is undoubtedly a master of his technology, and the new range of equipment he has designed is near to completion, upon which it should out-perform all of its UK competitors. However, he has a low opinion of customers, and regards them as not knowing what they are talking about technically. It's difficult to convince him that if the customers insist that our products are painted purple with orange polka-dots, then that is what we have to do. He knows better... definitely dangerous.

The production manager is rock-solid, no-nonsense, straightforward and easy to work with. Classic Glasgow.

The sales manager is a thoughtful, technically-aware, organised, presentable, cosmopolitan, quietly determined gent with whom I can work constructively.

The stock-keeper is working to the limits of her capability and we have far too much inventory, but that can possibly be reduced over a few months.

Enough assessment; time to get down to work. I'm commuting weekly so I work as a finance director during the day and process the purchase invoices by night. Quite apart from bringing the numbers up-to-date, this gives me a detailed view of the materials and services we purchase and at least some insight into our general relationship with suppliers (quite good, as it happens, despite the boss's necessary habit of not paying until the second reminder).

But given that we still have to complete the development of our new wonder-product and get it out into the market, we are going to need a six-figure amount of additional overdraft to get us to that stage. Nobody seems to have thought of the working capital requirement, and the necessity to have demonstration models of the new equipment. As a newcomer I have to rely to a large extent on the managers' estimate of how much is needed, and from experience I then double it.

Rather than meet the bank by starting from scratch, I prepare a one-page paper of the company's position, potential and financial requirements, agree it with the MD and give it to the bank before the meeting. This greatly shortens the meeting (the manager says "Ah, good; we don't need to take notes, then") and we emerge with our borrowing facility increased by over 30%. Now a lot happier, the managing director vacates her office for me to use, while she spends her time with her team working on the completion and launch of the new product.

The MD being widely respected in her profession, she is awarded an honour from Glasgow University, which gives everyone a boost. A couple of entrepreneurs from the south of England appear with a view to buying the company. There is a good possible fit: our strengths compensate for their weaknesses and vice versa, but as the interest progresses, the two of them prove to have greatly differing structural requirements: one wants to buy the company as a subsidiary and the other to create a trust. The possibility dies. A few others visit us, but without any real prospect of joining forces.

As the new wonder-product nears completion I examine the budget with a view to updating it. The cost of completion of the new product to production status has been under-estimated (isn't it always?) but not critically, and I turn my attention to updating the costs of marketing, launching, demonstrating and selling the product. We have a general cost for this in our budget, but we need much more accurate detail. I suggest hiring a display trailer set up as a clinic and publicising it so that clinicians can visit the trailer when it is in their locality and assess the equipment's capabilities for themselves.

At this point, the bomb is dropped.

The MD and the technical manager tell me that each clinician will want to take a sample unit away for typically two weeks to test it for a variety of clinical circumstances and uses before making a decision to buy a unit. Cue one very nasty feeling... how many trials do the MD and technical manager think will be needed to sell one set? The response is that about 10 trials will be needed to generate a sale.

That does it. The budget expects a sale of two units per month, which means that anything up to 20 sample units may have to be out on loan at any one time, with support from our technical personnel (additional vehicles and trained people will be needed, with travel and accommodation costs) and with transport from place to place, not to mention any maintenance of the loan or display models. Where is the massive cost of all these demonstration assets and related items in the budgeted balance sheet I have been given? And what will we use as funds to build 20 units before we even make a sale or two?

Deathly silence. Nobody has given any consideration to this. Nobody has mentioned at any time during the compilation of the initial budget that 10 two-week trials or thereabouts are expected to be needed for each sale.

I give the MD and technical manager two days to devise and present a plan for consideration. On the third day they admit that they will have to re-think their strategy entirely. They can still survive if they run the operation on a small scale until the sales are widespread enough to create enough demand from the medical market to support a proposal for additional finance, but it will be a slow process.

I have a private conversation with the non-executive director, who has devoted a considerable amount of unpaid time to the company and is equally annoyed that nobody has raised the issue of the massive amount of testing on third-party premises. After considering the entire range of possibilities we conclude reluctantly that there is nothing further that we can do, and we agree that I should leave the board immediately.

Sadly, I learn that the company ceases trading a couple of years later.

That is what can happen if you put principle ahead of practice.

LESSONS

A. *Keep your personal views and vendettas out of the business. Hiring one sex or the other on principle is ridiculous; you hire the most suitable people available regardless of personal attributes unless those attributes are likely to impact your business adversely. There are certainly very many roles in which females generally perform better, but that does not mean that one should hire an average female in preference to an above-average male.*

Moreover, as a clinical psychologist by profession, the MD should have known that her recruitment approach would not achieve the optimum result.

B. *Allowing the recording of purchases (or any other aspect of accounting) to be weeks late is ridiculous and even dangerous. Business leaders must be kept up-to-date with the real performance at all times, but the MD's prejudice against males was matched by her prejudice against all things financial.*

C. *Had the MD called for some intelligent planning and forecasting at an early stage, the board would have been immediately aware of the necessary size and cost of the marketing effort, and could possibly have arranged for the necessary resources to be available. That would probably have entailed close collaboration and possibly a degree of merging with another company, but that would have been preferable to struggling on alone towards failure.*

D. *If the highly personal issues had been subordinated to the technical and financial ones at an early stage, the company might well have been highly successful.*

23. GARAGE BANDS

There follows a strange period of coincidences in which various people loosely connected with the previous project kindly refer me to small potential technological start-ups. I am quite happy to advise them without charging any fees, because they are generally living off savings, with little or no income, and although their inventions are very different, the would-be entrepreneurs have some common qualities:

- they are highly intelligent and resourceful in their technological spheres
- they have great difficulty in describing what their products actually do
- they are equally vague about the benefits which the products will provide to their customers
- they are even more vague about the monetary value of such benefits

I give them what advice I can, especially on the subject of identifying and converting customers, and invite them to contact me with any queries, but nothing arises from these meetings. I'm not surprised, but I hope that at least one or two of them succeed.

One of the great drawbacks of small technology enterprises is that the entrepreneurs concentrate on features rather than benefits. The fact that a piece of technology can do something clever is of little consequence; what matters is how it improves the circumstances (which usually include the financial position) of the customer.

LESSONS

A. *Most of these technical players have some understanding of the niche for their inventions, but they don't have any idea of the size of the niche, and the financial rewards it can provide. Their energy and determination is directed mainly towards the technology itself, instead of the commercial qualities.*

B. *As a result of this, it is difficult to work with them to produce any form of business plan. They have clear ideas of what their inventions do, but no concept of how that can be applied to a money-making application.*

24. NOT-SO-HEAVY METAL

It is sometimes tempting when you're an interim between projects to take on a job that you're not really qualified to do. On the one hand that is unprofessional (possibly even illegal), but on the other hand *every* project contains elements which are new to you and therefore you have to do some learning in the course of every project. It's not something you can easily measure other than by instinct, but my rule of thumb is that the job should ideally be an 80:20 prospect; you should already know how to do 80% of what is required, and the other 20% you can learn as you go along, and it also helps to keep you on your toes. In that way, you can both meet the client's requirements and add to your skills with each project.

But this one smells like a 60:40... .

A large UK factory produces a wide range of a specific type of metal components for internal combustion engines, and is in need of a costing system to improve its inadequate knowledge of the profitability of its individual products. Fortunately the job is not going to start for several weeks, so I get myself some training material and do a large number of worked examples of standard cost variances, and draft a series of reporting formats and other pro forma documents. This (I hope) will enable me to hit the ground at least jogging if not running.

When the project starts, the first thing I learn is that there is a vast range (hundreds) of similar products, all of slightly different specifications. The introduction of full standard costing would be a colossal team exercise, for which the business has neither the time nor the money.

What to do? Somebody much brighter than I am points out that in each group of products there is one especially high-volume product, which is near the middle of the range in both size and production time. If we treat each of these products as the standard for its product group, we should have a relatively sensible answer. The variances should make sense for each group, and the costing of each individual product within each group can be weighted according to the amount of metal involved.

After consultation with the production manager and the engineering department we establish a high-volume "typical" product for each product group and we use this as the standard for that whole group. This of course means that we can only have variances for each product group, but if any group has a large overall variance a bit of digging will find the culprit product. This is crude, but it does at least give pointers in approximately the right directions towards the causes of the variances. Without a huge spend and a lot of time without a guaranteed commercial benefit, that is all we can do.

As with many interim projects, this one grows rapidly. Within a couple of weeks I've been tasked with designing a full set of monthly management reports showing the variances against the standards in each of the product groups, and a company-wide cash flow statement and balance sheet. With an agreed set of parameters this is a relatively conventional job in accounting terms, but when the first set of monthly reports are produced, there are howls of horror at some of the variances.

It is customary in such situations for the engineering staff to claim that the accounts have been incorrectly prepared, and there are certainly one or two quirks to be ironed out. However, the majority of the variances are reasonably verifiable, and the production team therefore set about identifying the specific products which have given rise to the variances. These wayward products take more than one set of month-end results to identify, but the variances are clearly being reduced and the accounting work begins to pay dividends.

The company is half-way through its financial year, and the group calls for a re-budgeting by the company for the second half of the year. This keeps me busy for a further period and allows some time to be spent on digging around in the balance sheet. There are an unusually large number of balance sheet accounts in the ledger, some of them of doubtful origin, and the budget requirement means that I can spend time on identifying assets of unlikely value.

Help is at hand by the arrival of a highly experienced no-nonsense controller from another division of the group, an expert who has an unerring instinct for where to find the bugs. With him pointing me at the likely danger areas, the cleansing of the balance sheet proceeds much more quickly, and we reach some more sensible figures. This in turn means that we can now place some reasonable reliance on the budgeted balance sheet going forward, but there is still a need for scrupulous monthly analysis of the results.

Without the implementation of a massive standard costing system that is as far as we are likely to get, and the budgeting and monthly accounting processes are handed over to the young accounting team, who are bright and keen to learn. I phone them occasionally from my subsequent project, to ensure that there are no skeletons left in the system, the budget or the report.

To my great relief the accounting team appears to be managing well, but neither they nor I get to know to what extent the variance analysis enables the production managers to pinpoint any sources of cost leakage. We have to assume that if there were any serious unsolved anomalies, the finance department would hear about it.

LESSONS

A. *Don't take on assignments that are on the very edge of your ability!*

B. *Once we got past the "pure" standard costing issues, however, I was back in my area of capability and produced clearly-structured and quite detailed overall financial information, which gave clear indications of the financial trends of the business and its individual product groups as a whole.*

C. *It was more than a little surprising that the factory, which was very large, did not have such information in the first place. It is not unknown for manufacturing businesses to be so focused on the products and their problems that the management forget that their real purpose is to make money.*

D. *While I was there, I received very little feedback on how the management viewed the results presented by my reporting package. However, that may have been because it took them two or three months to become acclimatised to it, and to use it to direct the business.*

E. *Although each of the variances reported by the system referred to a group of products, they did direct the management to the general area of the problems and were therefore useful. However, a fully-integrated standard costing system installed from the outset would have been the ideal tool.*

25. WORLDWIDE DISOBEDIENCE (PART 1)

The enquiry for this project has come in the last few days of the standard costing exercise, so without a break it's a drive to the station and a train to London. The meeting is in the Ritz, and I walk through the doors expecting to have to work my way through a crowded foyer, but there is only one man in an armchair, and he turns out to be my contact.

A world-wide industrial group has been formed via a private equity buy-out from a major European chemical group and they need a group controller immediately for an unspecified period. My interviewer is the global financial director. The plan is to parcel up various parts of the group and sell the parts individually to other groups at a substantial gain. Nobody seems to have asked why the original owners did not do that themselves, but I assume that they just wanted rid of the three non-core businesses without the hassle of marketing them around the world. They have marketed the three activities as a single group under the title "Specialty Chemicals" (US spelling), which makes three unwanted businesses sound quite sexy.

The interview is short and positive, and I head for King's Cross for a train north. I'm blissfully unaware until I get home that it is the last train out of there for several days, as much of the UK rail network shuts down with a major mainline incident. A few days later I'm on a Lufthansa jet heading east.

The head office has been established temporarily in central Europe and I am ensconced in a smart office in a well-appointed building swarming with other people involved in various aspects of the buy-out. The finance sector likes to use important-sounding terms and this is called a "leveraged buy-out", which, loosely translated, means that my client has paid well over the odds to buy three unwanted chemical businesses scattered across the face of the planet.

The package bought out consists of the following divisions:

- a bulk chemicals division, involving large factories all around the world
- a small-volume high-margin specific chemical sold through agents all around the world (this product turns out to be the real jewel in the crown)
- a single small but special one-customer application in Singapore

After asking around the head office, I receive a set of the financial results of the three divisions. The presentation of the numbers is brief and inappropriately laid out and of practically no use in running any division of any group. However, before I can get to grips with this subject I'm sent to another part of Europe to join an acquisition team. Our group is keen to show its backers that it will be active and progressive, and there is a product line available which the group believes would make a useful addition to the UK product range. I meet the team which comes out from the UK and we have 48 hours to access the selling company's information.

We are housed in a well-appointed boardroom with a huge range of information, ranging from technical to market to financial details and the team gets busy. I'm instructed to review the production costs and I refuse to do it. Why? Because the product, if purchased, will be produced on a UK production line with an entirely different cost-structure, and it is up to the UK production team to calculate the costs of making the product on the UK line.

The team tells me they want the European figures as a guide, but I still refuse. Human nature will kick in, and they will tend to work towards the European figures. They have to use UK figures or not at all. In the end the UK team say they can produce it at a cost allowing a decent margin and the purchase goes ahead with, I believe, successful results. I spend my time in the boardroom doing much more useful analysis of the seller's information.

Back to my office... before I can tell the group that I am not at all happy with the paucity of information available to the group financial controller, I'm told, much to my relief, that I am being transferred to a specific project. The worldwide payroll of the group (nearly 3,000 people) is to be transferred to revolutionary new software which allegedly will provide the following benefits:

- it will run payrolls for all of the 20 or so countries in which the group operates
- it will transfer employees' histories from one country to another whenever an employee is transferred
- on transfer, it will automatically apply the new country legislation to the employee
- it will thus maintain a full employee history throughout all of each employee's movements
- the company providing the software will keep it up to date with all changes in employment parameters in every country in which the client operates

The company developing this software is also based in central Europe. I watch the development with interest and no little scepticism, for the quantity of detail to be held is colossal, and requires even more detail in inputting and (worse) maintaining the parameters of each nation. The software company is by no means a proven outfit, and will put us in serious trouble if it hits any major difficulties. I get the impression that we are its first major client.

In the meantime, I am given another project, but before that starts, there is the worldwide managers' conference to attend.

The client group has over 20 countries in which there are mainstream operations, with factories in several of them. A large conference hall in central Europe is the venue and the group financial director kicks off the proceedings with a very lively and well-targeted talk on working capital. Nothing new, but very relevant to the occasion. He is followed by the group chief executive who amongst other plans says that factory managers will be incentivised on factory utilisation percentages, achieved by large batch sizes.

Is he utterly mad? For one thing, running a factory at near 100% utilisation is a very difficult technical proposition, and not a good idea. But worse than that is the result that managers will be pushing product through their processes to earn a bonus instead of *pulling* product through the factory to meet the combination of actual and forecast demand. Inventory will go through the roof, maintenance will lag behind schedule and bonuses will be paid in respect of inventory that has not been sold.

Worst of all, cash flow will suffer hugely. Factory managers should be incentivised on:

- on-time delivery to customers (less penalties for goods returned for quality defects)
- low inventory every month (this will act as a counter-balance to the delivery incentive)

We are then tasked with considering over lunch how the group can best motivate and retain its senior employees. I don't see anybody leaving the conference room with writing materials, so I take a pencil and pad myself. Half way through the meal hour the delegates at "my" table are still chattering about anything other than the remit, so I interrupt with an exhortation to get the job done. They don't pay any attention, so I say loudly "Well, money is obviously the most important factor."

That does it. They all protest loudly, claiming that money is not the prime motivation of the manager grades. So what is, then? Half a dozen vague intangibles follow, without the table actually agreeing on anything. Tired of the hot air, I write down a few of the usual clichés such as self-respect, job satisfaction and promotion prospects, but put "money" firmly at the top. I hand in the piece of paper with the table number, and never hear anything more on the subject because the conference runs out of time.

While the payroll company is developing its worldwide system I'm given the task of preparing and issuing a set of rules and responsibilities for the transport fleet in Europe. This is a worthwhile project as there is a large fleet of specialist trucks of various descriptions criss-crossing the continent and any sloppy procedures or missing paperwork can result in costly delays which can snowball, causing downstream deliveries to suffer when one delivery is held up. There's no use in delivering four chemicals to a customer if he needs five.

It's clear from the way the project is described that they consider it to be a major task. Fortunately they appoint an excellent administrator to help me. She has been in various admin roles and knows the rules inside out. We start by defining the stages of the transport operation from receiving an order to loading the vehicle to crossing borders to final delivery, and include all the possible hiccups, such as damaged product and border-crossing difficulties.

The task is then to fill in all of the possible occurrences under each stage of the delivery and return processes. In three meetings we have it completed and it takes up four pages of headings and bullet-points for actions, all written in the imperative mode. Two columns on the right define who is responsible for each step and the timing thereof (mostly "immediate").

The administration and transport managers are horrified. In true Central European fashion they are expecting a monstrous document, probably taking up a lever-arch file, and our four sides of A4 are a great disappointment. Eventually after they have challenged us extensively and been unable to find anything missing, they reluctantly accept it. Bureaucracy is alive and well in Central Europe. I thank my excellent colleague, who is the star of the show.

Now we come to the difficult bit. The group chief finance officer has decided that the group will use two third-party accounting centres, one in Europe and one in Australia (I cannot remember if the USA division was included in that; with 50 states all with different tax rates and rules, I suspect not). A colossal amount of work follows, and at HQ there is a large – in fact, huge – task force of senior managers seconded to the project and holding frequent meetings. The costs are colossal; they really must believe that they will save a lot of money by using that method.

At this point I have a showdown with the payroll company who show no sign of being able to complete their worldwide payroll processing product. On being pressed hard, the technical team admit that there is no chance of the payroll system being ready for when the group's two accounting centres are open. I then go to see the managing director to tell him that his company is fired from the project, and the predictable histrionics and pyrotechnics occur.

The ramifications of this are huge, and I'm not flavour-of-the-month with my client. But I didn't choose the payroll company, and I put up a strong case for each of our two dozen countries continuing to run and process their own payrolls, while I design and build a small top-end system which will give almost as much information on payroll and personnel as the originally proposed system. In fact, when implemented, it gives much more information, and very simply. It does not, however, track individual employee data, but that is readily available anyway, and transfers of employees between countries are very few in number, so that is no great loss.

I am assigned a Dutch payroll specialist who, once we get on each other's wavelength, proves to be a very capable facilitator with a quiet but hard-nosed and realistic attitude to what is and is not possible. He visits all of the group's countries to review their payroll facilities while I design the simple and robust group report package on Excel. The administrative director's secretary, who has never used Excel, learns how to use the set-up in a couple of hours of practice with dummy figures and a simple instruction sheet. She will also need absence cover, and that is arranged.

The Dutch payroll specialist does excellent work in masterminding the payroll accounting input process in the Europe and Australia accounting centres, and within our time frame we believe we are ready. Meanwhile, the group financial processing system goes live after 18 months of massive teamwork.

For some reason, throughout the regular progress meetings there has been considerable antipathy to my separation of the payroll accounting from the main accounting system, but that has died down and been grudgingly accepted. I have insisted that payment of the net payroll totals into banks throughout the world is done directly by the local controllers, and not through the payment modules of the new Europe and Australia accounting centres.

As it happens, at the first live month-end of the accounting centres the worldwide payments module fails and none of the supplier cheques is sent. But the 2,700 employees around the world have all received their net pay... suddenly I smell of roses.

Having disobeyed nearly every instruction I've been given and seen to be justified on all of those counts, I decide that I've gone out on a limb often enough, and my wife, who still vaguely remembers me, has booked a holiday in the Maldives. It is just after the Twin Towers demolition and the travel companies are practically giving away holidays, so we have three weeks in underwater paradise (at that time the islands are still relatively undeveloped).

However, just before I leave, they ask if I will go to Singapore after my return.

LESSONS

A. *Where do I begin? I never do find out how well the "leveraged" buy-out fares for the new investors, but having seen all the shenanigans as they happen, I have the feeling that the transfer to the new organisation has been much more expensive than planned. My own approach has been to run my own projects strictly under my own control with as few complexities as possible, for two simple reasons: I don't handle complexity well, and anyway, simple processes are less likely to have problems than complex ones.*

I also have a motto from my days as a working diver: always use the LOWEST level of technology that will do the job properly. While the rest of the buy-out team has been working on two hemispheric data processing centres, I've been working on a spreadsheet.

Guess which method is easier to operate?

And guess which method is less likely to encounter a problem?

B. *So many people and organisations LOVE complexity. Why? Does it make them feel clever or important? Does it enhance the status of the organisation? I think that the answer is a combination of these, and they're all wrong.*

C. *There are some areas in which you simply do not take risks, and payroll is one of them. The idea of putting the payroll on a brand new custom-built worldwide accounting system before the system had been well-proven was preposterous, but there was considerable pressure to do it.*

D. *Vanity plays an unduly large part in accounting and general management, just as it does in so many other walks of life. People love to boast about their sophisticated systems, but it is the end product which matters. A Ford Fiesta will get you through heavy traffic just as quickly as an executive BMW, and it's easier to park.*

It's much smarter to say "We have a very simple system which is easy to operate, tells us everything we need to know and doesn't break down" than it is to boast of a megalithic technical operation which costs you a fortune.

E. *Exactly the same applied to the rules for cross-border transport in Europe. They wanted a 50mm-thick manual, but they got four sheets of A4 which covered everything.*

F. *As the old mnemonic goes: "KISS" (Keep It Simple, Stupid).*

26. WORLDWIDE DISOBEDIENCE (PART 2)

The head of the Singapore operation is leaving, and I'm asked to stand in until a replacement is found. The group's bulk chemical factory in Singapore has been shut down and mothballed, but the Singapore company is continuing to trade across South East Asia in its three main products: bulk chemicals (obtained from other factories in the group, and stored in a warehouse at the docks), adhesives and a very special chemical application for which the only customer is a major international player in Singapore itself. My brief is to transfer the business to the group's Hong Kong subsidiary and shut down the Singapore operation.

The special application comes off the to-do list, because it only involves one specialist employee who is in firm control of his project, and he can be housed anywhere, as long as he remains in Singapore, close to the customer.

The bulk chemicals housed in the warehouse near the docks are the big issue. The Hong Kong team, who cannot wait to take over the operation, take this out of my hands by arriving unannounced and instructing the entire stock of chemicals to be loaded on to a vessel bound for Hong Kong.

Two of my clerical staff go to Hong Kong for a few weeks to help set up the transfer of the trade, and they are less than pleased. Singapore at the turn of the century is one of the best urban environments in the world, whereas (let me put this delicately) one could not truthfully say the same about Hong Kong.

The ship is being loaded, but there is a problem. The member of staff who is responsible for the inventory in the dock warehouse tells me that when loading the bulk chemicals for Hong Kong, the shippers have discovered a 44-gallon barrel of acetone which was not on the company inventory, nor on the cargo manifest. Apparently acetone is a substance of special concern.

A smallish gentleman with two not-very-small assistants arrives unannounced at the office, demanding to see the managing director. I introduce myself and we go into the meeting room... doors closed and no coffee, thank you. The two assistants sit at the far end of the table and the boss drapes himself in the top chair. Something about his movements, the fit of his clothes and his general relaxed demeanour suggests that if his two very tough-looking henchmen turned on him, he could leave them in a heap in the corner without breaking sweat.

He introduces himself as head of the Singapore drug squad. "Do you know how much heroin can be made from 44 gallons of acetone?" he asks quietly.

This is the big league, and it's not where I want to be. I explain firstly that I haven't the faintest idea how you make heroin, and secondly that when we bought the business as a whole, the stock records on the computer did not include the acetone. When the factory was closed down and the goods transferred to the warehouse at the docks (before my time), the acetone went there with all of the other chemicals. The staff checked the stock from the list to the physical stock, but not in the opposite direction, and thus did not find that the acetone existed, off-inventory, until they started loading the chemicals on to a ship.

To my relief he appears quite satisfied with the explanation and gives me a short discourse on the operations of the Singapore drug squad. It is very impressive, and the meeting concludes with my saying that I wish that all the countries in Europe would take the same approach as Singapore. He and his henchmen depart, polite to the end.

Phew... in spades.

I now have an empty factory to sell. The Singapore economy is suffering from the general depression in the Asia Pacific region, if not as badly as most of the other countries then still as badly as makes an empty factory difficult to sell. Moreover, it costs a lot of money merely to own it: by law we need insurance, security, maintenance, strict drainage control and a qualified chemical engineer paid full-time even though he has almost nothing to do. Naturally, he is scouring the region for a new job.

I obtain a new sale valuation for the empty factory and it's well below the balance sheet value. With the recession continuing, the value will continue to drop, and it is not predicted to recover for years.

Time to get in touch with the group's financial director. This whole conglomeration of companies was bought from a very large worldwide group in one of the ridiculous private equity deals which are all the rage at the time (finance is just as much subject to fashion as haute couture; such is the stupidity of intelligent people). We have to get out of this straightjacket.

I tell the group FD that to obtain the balance sheet value for the empty factory we shall have to maintain the office, the chemical engineer, various admin functions, a high insurance premium and the ridiculous rate of borrowing interest resulting from the ramped-up private equity deal until the time when (and if) we find a buyer willing to part with our net book value figure. Since there is no prospect of selling the factory at anything like the book value, we should sell it NOW to relieve the burden on the group.

Group financial directors don't like climb-downs any more than any other people do, but eventually I get the go-ahead and the factory goes up for sale. The price for which it eventually goes is well below the net book value, but there is nevertheless a very substantial cash saving, and we are relieved of a very sizeable slice of non-productive monthly overhead.

We now consider our revised position:

- we have a single individual who can do his development work almost anywhere
- we have an office facility into which we are locked for another two years and some months, with a very high penalty if we terminate the lease early
- we have a small specialist product range with a high margin which is sold throughout South-East Asia via an informal network of agents, and therefore requires very little central administration from Singapore (I visit some of these operators in the surrounding countries, and without exception they perform from a base of negligible overheads, looking after their

own financial affairs efficiently and causing us no problems whatsoever)

- we have massive tax losses brought forward, and have been advised that they can be set off against the two remaining streams of income, as they are all chemicals
- we have a sales director with wide experience of business in Asia Pacific, who has already demonstrated his worth as a general manager as well as a marketeer, and who has given me a considerable amount of help and advice throughout my stay
- buyers in South-East Asia generally prefer to deal with Singapore than with Hong Kong

As the saying goes, it's a no-brainer; this operation will be a long-running cash cow which needs almost no head-office management and will be sheltered for years by brought-forward tax losses. I have made a very strong recommendation to HQ to retain the business, but have heard nothing.

Twenty minutes before I have to leave the office for my flight home, with my extended visa expiring at midnight, I phone the admin director on the group board to interrupt their monthly meeting in Luxembourg. I wait expectantly while there is a muted discussion and then the admin director, who has been championing our cause, gives me the go-ahead.

Whoops of delight from the staff. The Singapore company lives on, and will make high tax-free profits on a small cost base for years to come. When the group comes to sell it, they will achieve a handsome sale price.

Taxi!

I'm sad to leave Singapore. At that time, around the turn of the century, it is probably the best business environment on the planet, and also a very pleasant place in which to live and work (and that comes from one who does not generally like cities). It is disappointing to see it now swamped with brash, overbearing buildings, a Grand-Prix circuit and many other out-of-character features. But that's progress, allegedly.

LESSONS

A. *I encounter the same hide-bound group management thinking regarding Singapore as I had met in Europe. If people only thought "We are here to make money" their thinking would be so much clearer. There should be no unnecessary structures, no vanity projects and no non-performing assets.*

B. *Even if a business has a clear-cut initial intention, if circumstances indicate otherwise the management needs to have the flexibility to switch to a more rewarding way forward. Businesses exist to make money, even if it means deviating from plans.*

C. *And talking of plans, remember that in this day and age plans tend to go out-of-date very rapidly, so be prepared to change your tactics in a hurry.*

D. *One of the major advantages of being a freelance operator such as an interim director is that you can stick your neck out without having to worry about your future prospects. It's much easier for an interim director to argue with a board than it is for a senior employee or even in some cases a full-time director. So if you're sure you're right, stick to your guns.*

27. EXTRUSION FUSION

Back in the UK, a former colleague who is now the managing director of a large and well-run metal extrusion company calls to discuss improvement of credit control and cash collection. The credit controller is a capable and experienced administrator and the company's product goes out on time and on specification, but the collection of debts from customers is a perennial difficulty. Can it be improved?

The credit controller sits in the finance department, apart from occasional spells as relief for the switchboard. I also sit in the finance department, as the MD also wants me to build a financial model for him, which means that I can be much more productive than I would otherwise be, merely shadowing the credit controller. She is clearly competent, so the likelihood is that a number of minor adjustments to her or other people's working methods are all that will be needed.

Surprisingly, over 30 points come to light, all of them small issues, but collectively impeding the cash collection process quite considerably. Rather than presenting a long narrative report I present about 30 recommended changes on three sheets of paper in a three-column landscape format: Observation, Implication and Recommendation. The following two examples give the flavour of the changes required.

Firstly, the credit controller sits in the accounting department, with whom she has various common concerns. But when I have her transferred to the sales office, she sits in the centre of the room with a salesman in each corner. She is thus *au fait* with all sales events without having to make any enquiries, and is able to query any circumstances or transactions likely to affect the credit situation. Similarly, the salesmen have her knowledge and experience on tap. The finance department is just across the corridor, so financial queries are easily answered, but it is the sales issues which are the prime concern.

Another change is the scrapping of the monthly credit control meeting. Instead she attends the weekly Monday morning production meetings, in which the credit situation of customers often has a bearing on what products are to be produced and when (there is normally no point in producing anything for a customer on credit-hold!). She also hears of production problems which may cause customers to delay payment. In this way, problems are reported, understood and resolved much more rapidly than before, to the benefit of customers and the company. The whole team knows the whole picture.

The other recommendations are in the same vein: small variations in procedure which make processes easier, quicker, harder to circumvent and more visible. What I like about this company is that they implement the recommendations immediately, so that we can check their effectiveness and make any adjustments accordingly while I'm still there.

Finally, as everyone concerned is already at full stretch, I go armed with documents to visit two customers at opposite ends of the country to resolve outstanding difficulties and return with two large six-figure cheques.

This is a company that is determined to get the best from all of its personnel and procedures, and so it is a pleasure to work for. Sometimes only a few tweaks are required to turn a good operation into an excellent one.

LESSONS

A. *Credit control is a front-line function, not a back-room one. For that matter, anything relating to customers is a front-line function.*

B. *Small adjustments to working methods can have a remarkably large effect on the efficiency of a department or function, especially when the adjustments relate to the customer relationships.*

C. *There are a host of reasons (some genuine, some spurious) why customers don't pay debts when they are due, and many of those relate to production. Examples include: wrong products, right products with faults, wrong packaging, wrong documents, wrong accessories, etc. The closer the credit controller is to the production function, the quicker any such problems are resolved.*

D. *In addition to being au fait with production issues, the credit controller must still be in constant liaison with the sales force and the finance team. There are many points throughout the business cycle which can affect the credit situation.*

28. FOOD FOR THOUGHT (OR NOUGHT)

A food distribution company is on the edge of insolvency. It has several depots around the UK, but the depot which houses the finance department is near where I live, and the insolvency practitioner advising the company's bank sends me in there to control the cash outflow. This is a daily process of reviewing the supplier balances and customer order levels, and determining the amounts and timing of the payments to suppliers.

It is fairly straightforward if a bit frenetic, but I still manage to get it wrong on one occasion and go briefly into forbidden overdraft. This brings me a deserved flea in the ear from the insolvency guru, but when I call the bank's main office to apologise, they seem quite relaxed. The guru has obviously smoothed matters over already.

A proposed restructuring is agreed with the creditors and providers of finance and it goes ahead. My very minor involvement ends at that stage.

LESSONS

A. A small percentage of companies in severe difficulty can be rescued, but in many cases action is not taken soon enough, with the effect that a company is already very close to closure when action is taken. The company is therefore put into an intensive care situation to ensure that it still operates according to the law until either a rescue is effective, or a rescue is proved to be not possible and an insolvency appointment follows.

B. Such an intensive care situation must be strictly controlled, so that no action taken by a bank, an insolvency specialist or any other involved party is in breach of the law. In particular, the rights of any creditors must not be compromised by anyone controlling the intensive care situation.

C. I have heard banks being criticised for taking the reins of struggling companies, but they do it with the intention of seeing if there is any chance of an ongoing business resulting from the mess. If there is, that can be to the advantage of the other creditors as well.

29. S-OX... MYTH AND GOLD-MINE

In the USA, acts are named after the senators who originate them. United Kingdom acts at least have titles that give some indication of their subject matter, but mention "Sarbanes-Oxley" to non-financial persons outside the USA and they are likely to be very puzzled.

Some major corporate crashes in the USA (Enron, WorldCom and Tyco for example) just after the start of the century (which began in 2001, not 2000, Tony Blair please note) shook the USA to the highest levels of government. How could these major corporations, presumably rigorously audited by the world's largest and most prestigious firms of accountants, have hit the wall despite having detailed state-of-the-art accounting and reporting systems?

I'll answer that question a little later. In the meantime, let us consider the panic reaction to these crashes (and no country panics quite as spectacularly as the USA; remember "War of the Worlds"?). As in any democratic country (totalitarian countries do things differently) there is a public outcry and calls for swift legislation to prevent a recurrence. Two US senators, Paul Sarbanes and Mike Oxley, lead the hasty enactment of the Sarbanes-Oxley act, an act which requires all US listed companies to document their accounting and control systems.

Thus begins a bonanza for the major and middle-tier auditing firms, overseeing and in many cases implementing this documentation for their clients. Within a year or thereabouts, all US companies and their subsidiaries, all over the world from the top to the bottom of the food chain, have full documentation of their systems, the quality of that documentation being somewhat variable.

Now, stop and think.

I mean seriously think.

Is that documentation going to stop a major corporate fraud?

Well, is it?

Of course it isn't. If a chief executive wishes to capitalise expenditure on an unsuccessful oil drilling programme as an asset instead of writing it off as he should, the transaction will go through the accounting system with all the required documents, instructions and authorisations. Joe Soap (or, more likely, John Doe) in the accounting department is not going to know that there is no oil in that particular block. Moreover, the bigger the failure is, the higher is the level of authorisation, and the less is the likelihood of somebody protesting or even querying it.

Never mind... this is monetary manna from heaven for the accounting and consulting firms. It's a pretty good time for interim directors, too, for there just aren't enough accountants and consultants to cover all of the documentation work.

Inevitably, all sorts of documentation methods are tried: laborious full narratives; simple notes; graphic layouts; flow charts, you name it.

Being at a loose end with no projects on the horizon, I phone the "no-nonsense controller" whom I met and worked for on project 24, with the innocent intention of joining him some time for a quiet beer, which we'd vaguely promised each other on that project.

But his response bears no relevance to beer: "Can you do a Sarbanes-Oxley implementation?" he asks. I answer in the affirmative, and in no time I'm on the road to central England, which the southern English quaintly call "the North", just as the southern Scots refer to the Edinburgh-Glasgow corridor as "Central Scotland". Do these people ever look at a map?

The requirement is extensive. My client (hereafter "the Boss") is responsible for nine manufacturing sites in Europe and one in South Africa, and the timescale is very tough. I'm introduced to his troubleshooter (hereafter "Lena"), a lady with a formidable knowledge of standard-costing-based manufacture, supplemented by a wicked sense of humour and a refusal to be fazed by any incident or instruction, no matter how ridiculous it might appear. Given that the group manufactures a vast range of vehicle components, those qualities will be valuable.

I ask for half a day to get my thoughts together. Any kind of narrative approach is a non-starter in view of the language diversity across

Europe, and anyway, graphics usually beat text when reporting on any kind of structural complexity. The answer is to use spreadsheets, their ability to lay out the controls in a clear visible structure being ideal. The steps in any system can be laid out together with columns for frequency, personnel and other data alongside the narratives, which should all be written in the imperative (e.g. "Sign all 4 copies of the despatch note and retain copy no 4").

A separate sheet can be used for each system or part of a system, giving rapid direct access to any part of the documentation.

Lena and I agree our format with the Boss, who likes it, and after a couple of modifications, off we go. I spend a few days trialling the approach in a small UK manufacturing unit who are genuinely very busy, but they manage to give me enough time to prove the concept. Within two days I have their purchasing system reasonably well documented (the world over, people tend to start with the purchasing system when examining a company, unless there is a pressing reason to start elsewhere; nobody has ever explained why). Back at the ranch, Lena is busy minimising her other commitments.

She has identified a Mediterranean site as the most organised and co-operative in the group, and we begin there (with the purchasing and payables system, as ever). Once we have the locals working on the project, we move on to an adjacent country, and again we get them started. They are not nearly as easy to get moving as the first country, and we realise that we shall have some problem children in the project, albeit that we have some sympathy for their having such a non-productive task forced on them.

It becomes clear that we'll have to split up and work independently if we are to complete the project within the timescale, and we divide the ten locations between us. The summer is then spent in offices, on factory floors, on aircraft, on conference calls, in meetings and at airline lost luggage desks. Two or three times a week we are on mobiles checking that we're taking the same approach to issues which have cropped up. Lena has previously spent a considerable length of time in one of the more difficult European sites, and her knowledge of the workings of the group is invaluable. We are thus working from the inside out, not from the outside in.

By the end of summer the product is a bit ragged, but it is

substantially there, and we can concentrate on tidying up the few remaining gaps. As the companies are all manufacturers with the exception of the European head office, we have been able to use the best example of each system's documentation as a template and check-list for the other subsidiaries.

Inevitably there are a couple of sites who drag their heels, whether because of other commitments or traditional continental antipathy to the British, I know not. Overall, though, the documentation is solid, although there is certainly room for continuing improvement when the documentation is reviewed by the sites each year. The main result, however, is that we're S-Ox compliant by the end of the project.

The UK/Europe head office team have a valedictory night in a pub near HQ and I head north the next morning with a slight muzziness in my head. The mobile rings and I pull in to the roadside. It is my S-Ox client (the Boss)... can I go to Spain for a couple of months to work with the deputy financial controller to bring him up to controller level?

Nobody refuses a job offer like that. But let's wrap up S-Ox first.

LESSONS

A. *Yes, we know that the concept is ridiculous. But if we're being paid to do it, and see a lot of Europe at the same time, are we worried? Nope. Nein. Nyet.*

B. *There are many ways of documenting systems for S-Ox purposes. There is one, however, which is much easier, quicker and more readable than any of the others: the spreadsheet file. It works as follows:*

- *one master data sheet, then a sheet for each major system*

- *a column for each of these 4 items: procedure number or reference, procedure description, date or time or frequency, person(s) responsible*

- *write each procedure as a command, e.g. "sign delivery note for acceptance"*

- *put a summary assessment at the foot of each sheet, plus any other relevant notes, such as improvements needed, proposed changes, etc.*

- *ensure that two or three people are capable of keeping it up to date*

30. THE LONG, HOT LUNCH-HOUR

The candidate for the controller's role in Catalunya is clearly made of the right material, which doesn't give me that much to do in the instructional field. However, the top-end financial documentation in that office, although competent, is somewhat clunky, so I can concentrate on automating and streamlining the apex of the information pyramid. This process has the benefit of highlighting various points which need more management attention, so the coaching fits in neatly with the reporting development. The candidate comes through strongly, not that there was any doubt about that.

Of much greater importance to me is that I discover The Spanish Secret. How on earth does such an easy-going, laid-back bunch of hombres (they are all male) run such a well-ordered business without any drama, grandstanding or aggravation?

It's the long lunch-hour.

Really... I'm serious.

They work until two o'clock or even later, and then stroll across to a very informal buffet area which is part of a large sports complex. Over an assortment of local foods, not separated into courses, they converse socially about anything under the sun. Holidays, movies, football, politics, films, etc., are discussed along with quality control, customer issues, production line hold-ups, staff promotions, any other business issues in no particular order, and pass the olive oil, please.

The result is that the tensions and formality of structured meetings are completely absent. The managers are quite open about their difficulties and volunteer to help each other with their issues. If nobody knows the answer to the problem, one or two people will volunteer to research the situation and come back with a suggested way forward. In this way, the lunch break lasts two hours or more, before they all head back to the factory and keep the promises they have made. And that third Villareal goal was *definitely* offside.

The Boss comes over from the UK for a general review and he also notices the atmosphere of laid-back co-operation. He says he feels guilty because in all his years with the group he has never visited the Spanish site.

I tell him that it's because he's never had a problem in relation to it. He nods and agrees; it's always got on with the job, presented its budgets and results on time, and done what's required of it.

I can think of one or two other nationalities who could emulate this mutually supportive approach effectively and some other nationalities who probably couldn't. It's very impressive, and the candidate achieves his promotion and slides seamlessly into his new role without needing any help from me.

I have become an españophile.

LESSONS

A. *There are many business cultures. Some tend to be national, such as in parts of Eastern Europe, while others can be entirely local. There is no reason why they should all be the same, so long as they all work. What this Catalan site has shown is that a relaxed culture can work just as (or more) effectively than a structured approach.*

B. *A culture is also dependent on the people involved. If you tried to emulate the above approach in another country or even in another part of Spain, you would find that it would work differently. But although different, it might work just as well. Why not try it?*

C. *The most obvious cultural differences I have seen are in forms of address. Fortunately, forms of address in the Western world have become much more informal within a business than they were in the 20th century, and I believe that is to the benefit of almost all businesses.*

Even most bank managers use forenames of clients once they become well-acquainted.

However, there are still many environments and countries where that level of informality would be regarded as highly disrespectful, so do be careful when in other cultures.

31. NO MORE IRON CURTAIN

There are many developments in process, and after the Catalunya sortie the Boss from the group has more work for me. My feet hardly touch the ground. A financial director has moved on from a large manufacturing subsidiary in Eastern Europe and I have a straight interim role in replacing him until a permanent successor is found.

Did I say "straight"? With the fall of the Berlin wall, the managing director of the site has moved seamlessly from deep socialism to high capitalism without batting an eyelid, a transition which appears superficially positive, but which makes for a huge network of political undercurrents within the business. The best defence as always for the interim director is stupidity (or at least apparent stupidity) because:

- in that mode you aren't regarded as a threat to anybody
- it requires no acting or intellectual ability
- if eventually you do have to put the boot in, it comes as a major shock to those who get booted

The MD has a sidekick of nebulous designation and even more nebulous definition of duties. He could best be described as the MD's Rottweiler. Fortunately I've learned from working in parallel with him on two previous projects that the only way to deal with him is to give as good as I get; if he's pleasant, I'm pleasant and if he's nasty, I'm nasty right back to him in spades. Not my preferred way of dealing with people, but you have to do whatever works best. For the purpose of this episode I shall call him Maurice.

The site has had a poor internal audit rating, with some 70 or 80 absent or defective practices to be rectified in a short timescale, and their S-Ox documentation, although technically adequate, still needs improvement. I recollect that I wrote much of it at this particular site, so I couldn't have done as good a job as I thought I had.

Plenty to get one's teeth into, and we get off to a good start when a very alert and capable newly-qualified accountant who has trained with an international firm joins our finance department, slightly against the wishes of Maurice. He likes terrorising women to the point of breakdown and is always on the lookout for more victims, and therefore wants her working somewhere less protected. Her induction starts with accounting for production, which neatly relieves me of one of my weak areas. The main body of the finance department is run by a group of intelligent, hard-working women, whose only need is some coaching and encouragement, which I provide when I can.

We grind our way through the scores of internal audit points, completing everything except the requirement for a fixed asset register, because the software which the group uses for fixed assets is not yet available in this country's format. We get clearance on our re-audit, and then it's straight into an updated budget. Only a third of the way into the year, and we're doing it again; that is how rapidly the situation changes in this industry.

The re-budget reveals a variety of calculation errors in Maurice's original budget, but he merely shrugs his shoulders and says "So?" when this is pointed out. Let it be said that if he found such errors in a subordinate's budget, there would be hell to pay.

Maurice's habit of persistently selecting a female member of staff and bullying her until she breaks down is in full swing, and we discover who his present victim is. As far as practicable, we remove her from his sphere of influence. I grind my way through the remainder of my stay, which ends with the news that a new controller has been identified and has accepted the company's employment offer.

At that point there is no further need to tolerate Maurice, and at the first appropriate point I give him a roasting. When he leaves my office I continue the tirade down the corridor. Entirely predictably, this results in an abusive phone call from his buddy, the MD, who is in Germany, and I give him almost the same treatment. He quotes the rule-book at me and I quote back some sections which over-rule his sections. After our contretemps he is reasonably respectful but Maurice continues his evil doings until word reaches us, many moons after the end of the project, that he has been dismissed for offensive behaviour. Not before time.

A somewhat turgid but nevertheless productive period of duty, enlightened only by a stream of humorous emails from Lena, comes to an end when the S-Ox documentation is passed by the internal auditors.

LESSONS

A. *The important feature for me was the solid back-up I had from the division office back in the UK. Working under a devious managing director with an even more devious side-kick as minister-without-portfolio (the two were made for each other) meant that the time inevitably came, fairly early, when I had to stop taking it on the chin and give them a roasting. So it was reassuring to have support from the group office.*

B. *Inevitably it is easier for a UK office to relate to conditions in mainland Europe than it is for a head office across the Atlantic to do so, and the US head office was not entirely aware of the amount of intelligent work put in at the UK office to keep the Europe operations moving in the right direction.*

C. *I was impressed at the calibre of staff in this former Iron-Curtain state, both in terms of their education and their practical performance. This may well have been because they had not been part of the Soviet Union itself. Their attitude to their work was impeccable, and whatever personal agendas they may have had, they did not let them interfere with business.*

32. FORTY DEGREES (ABOVE AND BELOW)

In many respects this is a repeat of project 31 for the same group, but further into Eastern Europe, in a climate that pushes plus 40ºC in summer and minus 40ºC in winter (I experience both, and strangely they give me the same burning sensation). Having worked on ships and offshore platforms in the Arabian Gulf, I'm used to plus 40, but minus 40 is harder to cope with, and that's without any wind-chill. The Cairngorms have never seemed that cold!

Curiously, on a farm a short distance from the factory, an ostrich lives outdoors through both summer and winter.

As the factory comprises over a hundred buildings, there is a considerable amount of time spent out of doors until the main management departments are eventually housed in a single building. A massive new computer system installation is in progress, with the most complex accounts chart I have ever seen, to cope with a highly complex standard costing system and the equally complex Eastern European accounting. Not comfortable territory for me.

There are three separate briefs:

- shadow and convert the somewhat wayward financial director into a satisfactory executive who operates in accordance with the group's rules and objectives, and who provides some leadership instead of being a solo act (in which he is casually comfortable, as his main staff members are excellent)
- ensure that the huge list of points from the failed internal audit are all fully rectified in time for the re-audit later in the year
- implement full Sarbanes-Oxley documentation, in which they have made no progress (this can be done partly in conjunction with the audit corrections)

The first brief dies within a couple of months. The financial director, despite his undoubtedly high intelligence, does not apply himself to either his specific job or any of the various projects under his wing. He also displays an increasingly contemptuous attitude towards the company and the group as a whole. He appears to consider himself intellectually above the group and its requirements, and his effect, if any, on his subordinates is negative.

After a short period of attempting to turn him round, I prepare a detailed report on the situation and he is eventually dispensed with. There are occasions when you know you're wasting time, and you shouldn't prolong them. A pity, but he is the architect of his own downfall, as the saying goes.

In complete contrast, the finance department itself is a vibrant and determined outfit. The controller is a dedicated young woman, a little highly strung, but that is entirely forgivable given the huge responsibility she bears and the number of conflicting requirements and views crossing her desk. The department staff (mostly women) comprise two distinct types of employee: youngsters with university degrees, strongly and determinedly focused on their responsibilities, and older people who have lived too long under the former communist régime to adapt to a modern commercial environment. Nevertheless, the older staff do a sterling job on the more routine processes of the finance department, but the better life they deserve will elude them.

The finance department provides me with a bright lad to deal with the S-Ox documentation, and once he gets the hang of the style and layout he begins to motor. I also give him the internal audit report, so that he is dealing with most of the identified faults simultaneously with documenting the procedures, avoiding duplication of effort. To avoid English language complexities, I tell him to write every S-Ox step as a command, e.g. "Sign goods despatch note for agreement with sales order", with columns opposite to specify the person(s) responsible and the timing. As often as practicable, we combine the audit rectifications with the S-Ox documentation in a single process.

This leaves me with the task of monitoring the huge plant's performance and ironing out the bugs which habitually crop up at month-ends. Big bugs, as it happens, involving hundreds of thousands of US dollars in value. The group uses an intricate standard costing system and at US level has a habit of ignoring large favourable variances in its subsidiaries but howling blue murder when negative variances appear, when some of these are caused by correction of the previous positive variances, which have been anomalies.

Standard costing is not a forte of mine, and the system used by the company is one of the most complex imaginable. Its complexity makes it hugely informative from a managerial standpoint, but also means that there are numerous channels down which information can be falsely directed. The system therefore requires continual husbandry in order to obtain the best information from it. The Boss back in England has to bail me out on a couple of occasions when I'm out of my depth.

After the blistering summer, and heading into the deep snow of winter, we are finally visited by the US audit team who comb through every part of our internal audit corrections and the S-Ox documentation. As the days pass into the second week of their visit, the tension mounts. Finally we are called into the boardroom and the US team give their verdict on both the audit remedial work and the S-Ox documentation.

We pass with a B+ grade, to everyone's relief except mine. The US team state that we would have had an A- grade if we had included summaries at the top of each accounting system in the S-Ox documentation. I point out that those summaries exist in full in the single overall top-end accounting systems umbrella document with which they have been provided, and I offer to show them the summaries so that we can be given an A- grade, but they don't want to know. They are already moving on to other matters. I'm still annoyed, 8½ years later.

The main concern, however, is that we have passed and are off the hook. The European controller is happy and I can wind up my work and head for home. It has been a tough 11 months, with my overnighting at Manchester airport on Sunday nights, flying to Warsaw then being driven for three hours to start work at Monday lunchtime. The first four days of each week have included evenings worked till 8 or 9pm, and the Friday has finished at lunch-time with another long drive back to Warsaw.

I have driven and been driven in many hairy parts of the world (Nigeria, Zanzibar and the Philippines come especially to mind) but I have never seen any driving such as in Poland. There are innumerable little shrines along the roads to mark where people have been killed. As we rocket past one very large stone-built shrine, my colleague and I ask our driver if that is a shrine for a very rich or important person. His response is "No, that was a bus-load".

Driving aside, I leave Poland with the highest respect for its people, especially the young ones coming through from the universities. The quality of their work and their dedication to their tasks I've found to be exemplary, and on several occasions I've had to bully them to go home when they have been putting in too many extra hours. The project has been a long, energy-draining haul through a very complicated organisation, but they have not flagged in their efforts at any time during my year there.

I have also received unstinting support from the team at the European HQ in the "North" (i.e. the centre, near the M62) of England, whose levels of assistance and guidance were never less than immediate and effective. Equally important, they all have a nice sharp line in cynical e-mail humour, which has kept me going through the darkest phases of the work. The new controller in Poland fits seamlessly into the frame, and is a robust character who gives as good as he gets.

All in all, a good project despite its many lumps and bumps. It is also the last project I do for that group. Whether there have been no more such projects or they're just fed up with me after three years, I'm too scared to ask. As work-mates they have been unparalleled, individually and as a team.

To finish on a lighter note, I'm impressed that some German customers visit us on 1st September and then a Japanese delegation arrives on 7th December. Is this someone's idea of black humour, or just my sense of the ridiculous?

LESSONS

A. *In the parts of Eastern Europe where I've worked, the standard of education and consequently the working ability of the younger peo-*

ple, who have not had to suffer a communist régime, have impressed me greatly. Moreover, their general knowledge of the world beyond their country has been greater than I expected; being mainly land-locked has made them more aware of the surrounding nations and events than their UK counterparts.

B. This was my 10th Sarbanes-Oxley exercise, and it was therefore a relief to be able to do it confidently in a much simpler layout. It also had a double use on this occasion, as completion of the documentation ensured that we were closing the gaps revealed by the internal audit, and also some gaps which had not been detected.

C. Even when preparing documents, it is often more effective to prepare them on MS Excel than on MS Word. If your information is largely tabulated, Excel is probably the more appropriate medium, and that goes especially for S-Ox.

33. HOME TERRITORY (NEARLY)

After a long gap following the year-long spell in Poland, I'm contacted by a recruiter for a project in lowland Scotland. A home game at last!

If I get the project, I'll be able to commute daily – pure luxury.

The company is part of a group which has several subsidiaries in the UK and Western Europe, mainly involved in manufacturing and selling a wide range of moulded plastic products (but not windows or doors, thank goodness). The group has been sold to a US outfit which has proceeded to centralise everything: central marketing, central sales, central product groups, central product research and development. Prior to that, each operating subsidiary had its own team of managers covering all of the necessary disciplines.

They are looking for someone to do a lot of linkage work while the group is being brought into its new configuration: group financial methods, group budget, group reporting, intra-group trading et cetera... conventional stuff.

The factory controller who interviews me is the most senior and most able controller in the group, a no-frills, no-nonsense gent with a well-developed sense of perspective and reality. He also has some group duties. At the interview he asks me a wide range of questions and includes the usual "How would you describe your management style?"

My answer is that I don't have one. Every person is different, and even a single person will be different from one situation to another, so there is no management style on earth which covers all eventualities. You therefore have to manage people according to their characteristics and the situation in which they are operating. You won't do very well with "one way fits all".

He seems OK with that and gives me more details about his operation, then asks if I have any questions.

"Just one" I reply. "You've described your company's very direct relationship with your customers and your ability to deal rapidly with any hiccups through your sales and technical and admin managers as your main strength. But now you have a group structure in which they'll be dealing with different people in different locations instead of having a direct and complete dialogue with you. Your main strength has been wiped out by a bunch of theorists. How do you feel about that?"

"Not good" he replies. "Not good at all. When can you start?"

The first and most important task is to build a group accounting model with related input schedules for the various companies. This takes up most of my time and the ball-game keeps changing as the newly-formed group inevitably keeps adding requirements for inclusion in the financial reports. The input documents for the operating companies are required to be easy-to-use; the simpler their job is, the easier life at the group office will be.

The group recruits a group financial director who is simultaneously knowledgeable, demanding and supportive, the ideal combination. Under his guidance the job proceeds smoothly, give or take the occasional last-minute amendment. We also have a co-operative group office who understand the parameters of the operating companies and whose demands are consequently practicable and reasonable.

This is generally unexciting but it makes a most enjoyable change, because I can concentrate on the task in hand without being diverted by any politics. Before too long we have the new group accounting framework operating with only a few hitches to be corrected. Instant satisfaction!

The next big task then looms: an integrated group budget. More modelling is required because of the new owners' decision to operate by department, so we have a group sales force, group research and development team, et cetera. This loads some complexity into the budget and also lessens the reliability of the budget as there is no track record for the costs of the new function-based structure, all previous costs having been incurred by each company. We go through several iterations until we are poised for the final run, eagerly awaited by the group management.

Now that I'm retired, my brain shuts down frequently and it doesn't matter, but when it shuts down two hours from the completion deadline of a group budget, that is a serious problem. For no apparent reason I cannot reconcile the budget, which I had designed to be self-squaring. A frantic gremlin hunt ensues. The group FD plays ball by resisting the temptation to phone me every ten minutes, but even though I'm left in relative peace to make attempt after attempt to square the damned thing, I cannot do it. I have clearly over-ridden something which should have been protected, but what?

Eventually, my head spinning, I leave the office and wander twice around the factory grounds slowly, trying to think of anything but the budget. With about 20 minutes to spare I return to the office and to my huge relief the budget squares at the first attempt. I cannot even identify what I was doing wrongly. My relief when I phone the group FD and say "It's on its way" mirrors his, and afterwards we can have a laugh about it. However, I suspect that his bad moments were even worse than mine.

The group now has a complete financial reporting structure, and a lively and intelligent group finance office, based in Lancashire and very supportive.

Job done... and some time later I have a Chinese dinner with the local controller to make sure that I haven't left any skeletons lying around in the closet. He informs me that the group operational structures have been abandoned and that the operating subsidiaries have gone back to looking after their own products and customer bases.

Quite often the people on the ground are a lot smarter than the people at high altitude. But please don't quote me on that.

Thank goodness we had a highly intelligent, supportive and experienced group financial director who could handle all the changes at high level, and a local controller whose antennae were always well-tuned and fully functioning.

LESSONS

A. *When a subsidiary company has the complete range of personnel, including marketing, sales and product development, it is in a position* *to satisfy its customers' requirements promptly and completely. Relationships are generally easy to maintain and so is the vital understanding of the customers' preferences. That does NOT prevent the company from being an effective member of its overall group. One can be self-contained AND a team-player.*

B. *If you are proposing to centralise various functions for the sake of centrality, economy or knowledge pooling, be very, very careful. Business is all about the front line, and good head office leaders understand that.*

34. ON COURSE, OFF SITE

The course material I used on project number 6 (the business stationery company) was a modification of a similar course I'd run for various companies, adapting the material only slightly. The attendees have to work their way through various examples of profit statements, cash flow statements and balance sheets, the numbers being deliberately chosen to show how a profitable business can slide into a disastrous cash situation.

Non-financial managers can get to understand the differences between profit and cash flow quite quickly. What puzzles them is how a balance sheet works.

The course also includes a session wherein the candidates build a balance sheet by 12 consecutive transactions, all mapped out in columns on a single landscape sheet of A4 paper, with a rudimentary profit statement at the foot. By actually building the balance sheet from scratch, they finish the course with a straightforward appreciation of how it works and what the effects are on the position of the company.

In this case the company is a major food-processing company whose financial director is constantly urging her colleagues and staff to better efforts. We tailor the course slightly to her teams' needs, she obtains a very suitable location just far enough away to prevent managers from slipping back to the office, and the course runs well. All of the traps hidden in the figures are sprung, and the learning points taken on board.

We run the course for more of the staff a few years later, the difference being that the company now has its own training centre on site. Although the candidates are genuinely trying to stay with the course, the presence of business issues only just across the car park is too much of a temptation and the course does not have quite the same intensity as it did on the first run.

LESSONS

A. *The lessons from the course in project 6 apply equally here. We ran the course off-site and it worked well, with high satisfaction levels from the attendees. Doing it this time at the company site is somewhat less effective; there are too many distractions and the ambience is much less concentrated.*

35. HOW NOT TO DO IT

Once upon a time there were two large UK companies who made domestic products which were similar in use, but distinctively different in appearance. The products were simultaneously functional and aesthetic, and both companies gained deservedly strong reputations around the world for the high quality of their products (style and robustness). The product ranges were extended from the expensive qualities to middle-range items, both levels being bought in large quantities world-wide.

The two companies eventually joined forces, and various other product ranges were added to the group, while the group structure itself became more complex.

But consumer tastes and attitudes changed, increasingly rapidly as people began to live their lives very differently in the late 20th and early 21st centuries. The products retained their worldwide reputation for quality and distinction, but the demand for them weakened steadily. The companies then added less up-market, more utilitarian products and a much wider range to fill their capacity. These were not nearly so successful and the diversity of output very probably weakened the main brands. When potential customers see up-market brands alongside populist products their estimation of the higher brands often declines, sometimes dramatically.

This is where and when we start.

It is a classic example of how slopes become slippery.

Although the two companies have merged their operations to some extent to reduce costs there is visible friction between the two camps, particularly at senior executive level, where a degree of partisanship persists. I shall refer to the two companies as Driver and Wingman, and their chief executives as Mr Driver and Ms Wingman, which roughly aligns with their apparent status. Mr Driver is erratic, illogical and irascible and Ms Wingman appears to be conventional, sensible, loyal and hard-working. However, both of them seem to be out of their depth when faced with changing customer tastes and the necessity to realign their operations.

They are due some sympathy for that, as the operations which they have inherited are over-complicated in almost every respect, exacerbating nearly every problem they have. ·

The chairman responsible for both businesses and their other less prominent subsidiaries or associated companies is well-known for various personal achievements, and is a prominent figure in the world of high-profile companies. This kind of prominence typically increases when such well-known companies hit trouble, but it is not apparent in this case. Is the chairman working hard behind the scenes? Very probably.

There is also a deputy chief executive (in name if not in title) who is based a few thousand miles away, but who takes a more visible role than the chairman in steering the two companies.

In some matters herein, Driver and Wingman are considered separately and in others they are considered as a joint matter. This is inevitable as some of their activities, such as production and marketing, are carried out jointly to some extent. In fact, "to some extent" defines almost every quality of the group and every situation it faces. "Definite", "Complete" and "Co-ordinated" are not adjectives that come to the surface on this project.

On the positive side, the group has hired an energetic financial director (or possibly controller, but he operates at director level and punches well above his weight) and a greatly experienced consultant who has wide and deep knowledge of the industry. I am hired to work for the consultant on the financial side, and find him to be practical, pragmatic and personable. Not only is he an excellent leader, but he also works well with the new financial director. They are both at the highest level in the interim director market and deserve to be listened to very carefully (which they aren't, much of the time).

There are two other personnel on the crisis team, one on information systems and the other on logistics. The two main companies have never had their computer systems linked, with the result that the computer department spends much of its time transferring and checking data from one company's system to the other, leaving little if any time for desperately-needed systems development. The logistics position is even worse, as neither company appears to have pruned its product range for a very long time. The number of products apparently in inventory is colossal, ranging from the expensive élite to the everyday trivial, and must be very confusing for potential customers out there in the public, let alone the management of the two companies.

There are many other disjointed arrangements. For example, the main UK store is computerised, but the containers used for the products are unique to UK, and unusable internationally. Thus the batch quantities in the storage computer system are similarly out-of-step with the imported quantities.

The other (very) major factor is that much of the production has been transferred to a state-of-the-art factory in Asia Pacific. That factory is modern and appears to be efficient, and has considerable room for expansion in its grounds. There is therefore much sensible discussion on the viability or otherwise of transferring the entire UK output to AsiaPac.

On my visits there I have considerable difficulty in obtaining quality time with the AsiaPac managing director and financial controller; at first this appears to be because of their considerable work-load, but latterly I have an increasingly firm impression that I am being frozen out (an occasional hazard of being an interim). However, there is little doubt that this is a well-run and capable facility, and a suitable base for expansion. The one large cloud on the horizon in this part of the world is that another AsiaPac country is selling corresponding products of similar quality at a notably lower price, on the back of very low labour costs. Being new to the market, however, it does not yet have such a solid reputation.

Despite my inadequate degree of contact with the AsiaPac controller, we manage to prepare an apparently reasonable first draft of the budget for the forthcoming financial year.

Back in the UK, the deputy chief executive (or deputy chairman; clarity is not a feature of this group) calls a meeting of 20 persons around a long table, he and Ms Wingman being at one end and Mr Driver being at the other, which is not an accident. The two company heads cannot tolerate each other. I am seated at the midpoint of one of the long sides, my head going from side to side like that of a tennis spectator. There is no apparent agenda, and the discussion wanders round like somebody lost in a maze. When the subject gets around to the question of putting all of the production into one factory, somebody mentions that the unused ground adjacent to the AsiaPac factory is ideal building ground.

The deputy chief executive says "Well, why haven't you started digging?"

There follows an embarrassed (or at least bewildered) silence. Deciding that enough is enough, I lean forward and say "We haven't started digging because you haven't approved the project."

Somebody titters (Ms Wingman, I think) and the awkward silence continues for a few seconds. The discussion returns to vague practicalities (and a host of impracticalities) but by the end of the meeting, of perhaps two hours' duration, not one single major initiative has been agreed, even tentatively.

Not impressive. In fact, very hard to believe. Did I really sit through all that?

My consultant boss gets me to work on a sensible UK budget, working with a very experienced management accountant who does a wide range of excellent work, greatly appreciated by the financial director and almost ignored by the remainder of the management, who don't appear to relate easily (if at all) to numbers. The management accountant and I are instant compadres, having been raised in the same distant part of the world. After review by the controller and some additional instructions, the management accountant's budget starts to look like solid sense: tough but achievable.

Later, Mr Driver predictably gives me a telling-off for my comment about the digging, but I point out that someone had to bring the meeting back to sanity. He and Ms Wingman are hardly on speaking terms, and he becomes increasingly irascible and irrational. One day he calls a senior meeting at 0900, but not including the financial director, despite the topic being heavily financial. I sit through the meeting with my laptop, awaiting instructions or at least a few pearls of wisdom. Eventually I send an email to the absent financial director saying "The time is 1030 and we are slowly but surely inching towards item number one on the agenda".

He is still chuckling when the meeting ends hours later with nothing much decided.

The inventory is colossal and the team leader has brought in a very sharp Antipodean to perform a review of the product range. This is so huge and so ad-hoc that the newcomer is working over 20 hours per day and before long becomes seriously ill, spending some time in hospital in a critical condition. Fortunately he does recover and his work proves to be of considerable importance. But that's not to say that anybody in the business acts upon it.

Amongst his findings it appears that in order to generate enough sales to keep their jobs (and if relevant, earn some bonuses) some of the salespersons are inflating their sales forecasts. Each product has a minimum production quantity and many of the orders generated are below the production levels. The sales force therefore appear to be increasing their forecasts to levels at which the products will be manufactured, and even if only some of the "forecast" products are sold, those sales will be attributed to the sales persons. They are therefore working hard on increasing the inventory and the corporate debt.

The next thing that happens is that the financial director is dismissed, without any announcement or even a confidential word to those of us on the interim team (or consultancy team; you could use almost any definition). I call the director at his home and ask what personal effects he has in his office, then remove them that evening and take them to his house. The next morning somebody notices that his office is substantially empty (although the company items all remaining are clearly visible) and there is an immediate office-wide panic in the belief that there has been a burglary. Eventually I hear about it and put them at ease.

As the financial director was the only person in the high-level structure who had any consistent understanding of the group's requirements, those of us who remain carry on with our tasks in the knowledge that we will not achieve much. I complete the budget thanks to a huge amount of input by the costing accountant, and we hand the budget over to the financial accountant, a sensible and capable official who has worked well with the recently-departed financial director. He reviews it and confirms that he can run with it (albeit knowing that the parameters are likely to change before long).

The consultant and I wrap up matters as tidily as we can, as with the financial director out of the picture there is nobody else with whom we can work. Mr Driver, who exists in his own impenetrable bubble and seems to be senior to Ms Wingman, instructs us to go when we consider that we have finished.

Many years later, the brands are still selling. This can only have been done with massive external reconstruction and funding, with an entirely new high-level management. Putting in an ad hoc collection of interim directors and mid-level specialists was only ever going to scratch the surface of such a vast international range of problems in a disjointed operation which was going in several different directions simultaneously.

The top-level management should have been replaced long before the meltdown.

Stop press! As this is being written, the chairman, a worldwide figure of note as both a businessman and a sporting star, has been declared bankrupt.

LESSONS

Where on earth do I begin? The many major mistakes had been made and exacerbated long before the team of which I was a member arrived on the head office scene. The US Cavalry arrived much too late, which is in itself a learning point.

A. *Combining two businesses selling similar products to a similar range of markets is unlikely to succeed without careful stewardship of the different brands. If they are clearly different, there may not need to be much need to prune or amend either range, but if they are too similar in appeal, each is likely to impact on the other. In this group there was no visible strategy for maintaining the separate appeals of the different brands.*

B. *Moreover, there were a considerable number of other products supplementing the main ranges, and these ranged from exclusive ultra-high-quality items to mass-produced products, some of them based on or linked to popular cartoon characters or other fictional types. Some of the more mass-market items appeared to be bought-in, and even if that were not the case, it gave the companies a mass-market image which would be likely to deter potential customers from buying the high-margin items.*

C. *It was probably wise to maintain the two major companies as separate entities to protect their strong brand images, but the managing director of each company should have reported to a single overall chief executive. The situation which existed had one managing director able to make decisions over the head of the other, which created considerable bad blood, and did not ensure that decisions were made for the good of the whole group.*

D. *The executives themselves did not appear to be of the calibre required for such large and prestigious organisations, particularly in an era of difficulty. Moreover, the somewhat nebulous group board overseeing the main company executives did not give any clear direction, nor did they appear capable of doing so.*

The above lessons are necessarily generic. To go into detail would require another book, and one day someone somewhere may be inclined to write one, albeit for a limited readership.

36. THE DREAM TEAM

The interview for this project goes conventionally over a bite of lunch, and then finishes unconventionally. The group managing director wants a reference from someone for whom I did things well, and also from someone for whom things didn't go well. Machiavellian! It makes a refreshing change of approach. I short-circuit the process by introducing one former client who has suffered me at both my best and my worst and he appears to satisfy the MD.

In this project I take over from a financial controller (doubling as company secretary) whose financial knowledge and skill are remarkable and whose work is impeccable. Sadly, that has been his downfall for a variety of reasons, the main two being a lack of flexibility resulting from the insistence on doing everything impeccably and very late financial results for the same reason. The monthly figures are not materially correct; they are correct.

The company imports and exports a commodity with a degree of processing involved, and has a reasonable percentage of the world market therein. Considering the relatively small number of personnel involved, this is impressive (to me, anyway). With the exception of the two IT staff and yours truly, the entire UK clerical staff (mainly marketing) and the group managing director are in a large open-plan first-floor office. The product is handled in the downstairs warehouse, with processing contracted out.

The company has various offices in other parts of the world, but my immediate task is to get control of the accounting at HQ. In introducing me to the two dozen staff, the MD's PA, who seems to know everything there is to know about the business, describes the very quiet and unassuming management accountant as "our Elvis impersonator", which I note for future reference. Anyone who can remain as unobtrusive by day and yet arise to impersonate The King by night has got what it takes.

Yes, the accounting is immaculate. The purchase ledger clerk does most of her work at home, where she has commitments, and is only in the office part-time, but the purchase invoice processing is impeccable. So is everything else, it appears. So why are the results for May not published until early July? There is no real answer, other than a culture of getting every last transaction correct. Admittedly, the figures from various overseas offices take some time, but they are mostly small beer, and can be absorbed accurately enough in advanced draft form without distorting the overall figures.

After my first month-end we have a finance department meeting, in which I tell the team that the monthly results will in future be needed in full on the third working day of every month. That is less than one tenth of the time currently taken.

Horrified silence... then they start asking how on earth it can be done.

The secret lies in the many things which can be done before the month-end. Fixed assets, payroll and creditor payments are all in our control and can be completed before the month-end. The bank accounts can be reconciled on the last day and if necessary adjusted for any late event. And so on... most of the obstacles to rapid processing and accounting aren't really obstacles at all; it's just that nobody has seriously considered whether there is a more efficient way of dealing with them, and whether the small items can be ignored (or at least estimated to an appropriate degree of accuracy).

I hand them out a copy of an end-of-month planning matrix and we discuss how to use it. We also decide (very easily) who is responsible for each part of the accounting systems and who is the back-up for each section during holidays, illnesses, etc. The team looks a bit bemused, but they go to work enthusiastically and eventually come up with a practicable matrix.

The big hurdle is that they must do two month-ends, one immediately after the other, to get aboard the train. Their instruction is to get the earlier month "reasonably accurate" without sweating the small stuff. For example, there is no need to reconcile the bank for the first month, nor to reconcile fixed assets or supplier accounts or customer accounts, provided that everything is reconciled fully at the end of the second month.

The team pitches in with a huge effort and come the next board meeting we have two sets of monthly results, not one. Inevitably the numbers are slightly rough and ready, but from now on they will be accurate and we shall be having board meetings in near-real time, not in distant retrospect. I should mention that our overseas offices have also been subject to this telescoping of timescale, but they are much smaller operations and they cope well with the requirement.

The hound-dog accountant in particular has done an impeccable job of speeding up the processes, and I ask to see his CV. It is very out-of-date, so in the evening I re-write it and show it to him the next morning. He likes it, to my relief, so I ask for it back as I want to do some further work on it. The following week I give him a revised CV as a financial controller and give him three months to achieve that level. Not very risky; he's bound to do it. Indeed, he is already running his department in a very business-like way and is impacting more on the other departments, to their burgeoning respect.

The next major project is to prepare a budget for the forthcoming financial year. As my predecessor has been an immaculate accountant, that is not too difficult, but in addition to his groundwork there is a wealth of untapped material in the sales ledger system. The greatest single omission in financial control in almost every company I've seen isn't failing to examine the overheads in detail, it is failing to consider the sales and cost-of-sales in detail. That is the beating heart of the business.

The sales ledger clerk analyses the entire customer list by product group, currency, credit period, internal or external agent, sales staff responsibility and finally, from the sales director, the budgeted quantity and value of product for the following year and the expected net margin percentage.

The chairman, managing director and I project this on to the board room wall and play with the numbers for days. The expertise lies with them; I'm merely working the model. Could we chop out a large proportion of low-margin customers without serious loss of net income, and spend the time on higher-margin sectors, some of them in particular? Could we better match the currencies of our raw materials with our sales currencies? Do the workloads need to be better balanced amongst the sales staff?

We slice it and dice it for three days and involve the sales staff, until we have a very clear view of the way forward. That's not to say that the markets will co-operate with our intentions, but we will be well armed to cope.

A group of customers appears on the analysis with much higher gross margin percentages than any other customers. Who and what are these? I'm told that "That's just sector X" (I cannot divulge the details of the sector). Who is in charge of sector X? Nobody, it turns out.

This is a classic example of people concentrating on sales instead of margins.

The immediate command is for someone to research and provide contact details and background for every sector X company in Europe by next Thursday, and the rest of the world by the next-but-one Thursday. Specific high-experience salespersons are to be put on the case. There is gold here to be mined, if we dig in the right places with the right tools.

The accountant, who has been a driving force in his quiet way, is later promoted by me with the MD's agreement to financial controller, and is worth every penny. Because they are working with recent transactions only, the finance department are now on top of their work as opposed to wallowing in it and their status in the company rises. We already have an excellent systems team of one extrovert and one introvert, so all that remains is to find the ideal financial director. We're getting there.

Previously we have been interviewing for a full-time finance director, but the additional momentum now provided by the finance team means that only a part-timer is needed. Someone with all-round commercial experience and a shrewd mind who can give us a few days per month is the target. Our head-hunters present their first offering, who gives us his background in a confident, relaxed way which causes the MD to catch my eye. The MD starts his side of the story, and after less than two minutes the candidate interrupts gently and says "I like you guys. How about it?"

I stand up casually, say "I'll leave you two to sort things out" and exit the room. If everything were that simple, I'd never get any work. The new man proves to be ideal: a robust, no-nonsense pragmatist who has been round the block more times than most.

All that remains is a visit to two of the company's offices in other parts of the world. In the first one we are just as lucky with our recruitment as we have been in UK, and in the second country we have to put a business to bed. Again, the person responsible is pragmatic and efficient, and the only tricky task is forecasting on a cash basis the future income and costs of running down the business. In such cases, speed is usually of the essence, because if you hang on to get the best possible prices for assets sold, you almost inevitably incur more additional costs than the extra sale value. Our local man is of the same mind, and does a fine commercial job.

The reader will note that I have not mentioned any major problems on this project. That is because there aren't any. Well, not for me, anyway. Effective chairman, pragmatic directors, efficient finance and IT staff, enterprising sales staff and an outstanding executive secretary/ office manager with 360º radar and a wicked sense of humour make this a job to remember. They just need a few tweaks here and there to move from a very good outfit to an excellent one. I do the tweaking; they do the work.

I wish there were more like them. I really miss them.

LESSONS

A. *In functional terms, the big howler was having late monthly results, just for the sake of getting numbers exactly right. To keep the business momentum going, you need sensibly accurate results within a couple of days after each month-end. See chapter 1 for another example.*

B. *In strategic terms, the main problem was the age-old one of focusing on sales instead of margins. A few high-margin customers are worth a whole slew of low-margin ones, usually with a lot less effort once you have the relationship established. Once we had identified a specialist high-margin customer group, that sector had to become the main target.*

C. *In human terms, this project proved that you don't need superstars to run a high-performance company. Sharp leadership is necessary, but for the staff in general, it's the old cliché of "work smart rather than work hard". A certain cussedness and refusal to be beaten are also helpful. The staff of this company had all the right qualities; they just needed their forward path to be a little clearer.*

D. *I've noticed that certain areas of the UK perform better than others in running a profitable business, partly because they respond more positively to ideas. The two areas I've found most responsive, with only a couple of exceptions, are the M62 corridor and Greater Glasgow. Both areas are up-front with their thoughts, making it much easier for outsiders like me to understand their main issues and work with them constructively. Other areas please note... be forthright with your information and considered opinions!*

37. SAME AGAIN? NO!

This project is within an hour and a half of where I live, so I have the unaccustomed luxury of going home every evening.

The office layout is virtually identical to that of the previous project. *Déjà vu*: managing director and efficient blonde PA in one corner, the boardroom behind them, finance department in the parallel corner, a big open-plan work area with four time-zone clocks on the wall.

Spooky.

There the similarity ends, however. I have been brought in by the chairman to bring some focus to the operation, which is becoming too large and fragmented to continue on its current ad hoc basis. But the managing director is more than a little difficult to pin down on anything, and getting a firm decision on any financial matter is nearly impossible.

It works like this. The company takes in many types of used portable electronic equipment, the staple diet being mobile phones. These are sorted into workable quantities of each type of product and then sent to various companies in other parts of the world for reconditioning, after which they are sent to the most appropriate destinations for sale to end users. Typically there is strong demand in countries of lower disposable income. I should mention that the client's local team also do some reconditioning themselves.

The MD attempts to head in several different directions simultaneously and has me preparing a variety of financial models, none of which ever gets completed. I suggest to him that we concentrate on the most important one, viz the one which will generate the earliest net cash inflow of any reasonable size, but he continues to vacillate.

He also is critical of the finance team, who are actually well in control for the most part, their only areas of difficulty being his various forays in other directions, usually with minimal briefing and maximum potential for diversion. His team, however, is clearly capable, their only problem being him!

Eventually I have a short discussion with the chairman. We agree that if the MD is going to have so many projects on the go, he should bring in a full-time financial director. That happens fairly quickly and I return to a state of sanity.

The good news is that the company is eventually taken over by another concern, and expands successfully in an organised fashion. No input from me there, but they're a good bunch and I'm delighted to hear of their success.

LESSONS

A. There are definite lessons from this outfit, but they're difficult to describe. It's not the first time I've met a managing director trying to take a company in several directions at once. There's nothing wrong in having several goals, but you have to rank them in order of advantage and also in order of possible completion. Once a practicable sequence of events has been ascertained, the management need to get on with it, and put the other ideas aside until the early goals have been achieved.

B. Given that the purpose of a business is to make money, any managing director who derides or downgrades his finance team is heading for trouble, or at least failure to get the best out of his business.

38. THE BOOK

There are occasionally gaps of a few months between projects, especially more recently as there are many more interim directors in UK than there were when I started out. I take advantage of such a gap to complete "The Financial Controller", a book I have been writing on-and-off over a couple of years. It is a much larger book than this one (about 400 pages).

There are hundreds of books about company finance, statutory accounting, law, auditing, selling, directorships and other financial facets of businesses, but almost nothing about the overall running of a business. I have therefore, in between projects, been compiling a book on the entire scope of work of a typical industrial financial controller. It covers the people, the systems, the structures, the organisations, the external parties, the information, and concentrates heavily on the practical aspects. It is theory-free.

After many months of writing and editing, the book is launched in 2010, and gradually begins to attract attention. Agonisingly slow at first, the sales go on an upward curve and increase year-by-year. They are now in the thousands, and as the book will almost never become outdated it should continue to sell.

To my surprise, I find myself referring to it more than casually. I've had a good run, and if I'm becoming so forgetful that I need to look things up in my own book, then it's time to think about calling it a day. A couple of projects more should take me to the age where the government starts paying me for a change, and these projects do turn up.

LESSONS

The book itself contains the lessons! However, if you are going to write a textbook, I recommend this sequence:

A. *Determine who are your likely readership and what they will want (remember that want is more important than need – they may need advice, but if they don't want it, you won't sell it).*

B. *Set out your main answers to their wants, determine the sequence, and start writing; do the easy bits first and as you gain confidence and fluency, the difficult bits will become easier, and if you hit a block, take a break.*

39. SHARED SERVICES

When I first heard of the concept of a shared service centre many years previously, I thought it was a ridiculous idea. But since ridiculous ideas are sometimes the best ideas, I chided myself to keep an open mind on the subject.

When I did start working for companies using shared service centres, I was taken aback by their efficiency. In some cases I had no contact whatsoever with the centres, but in others, particularly the case of the centre in Australia when I was in South-East Asia, there was a good deal of dialogue between the centre and me. The most impressive feature was the ability of some of the people in the centre to understand quite a bit about the business merely from the documentation which they processed. That's genuine intelligence.

So I'm intrigued when a former colleague (the indomitable Lena) who is now involved in the running of a UK shared service centre asks if I'm interested in doing some structural work for it. They need some documentation of their various responsibilities to give clarity amongst their own departments, and to ensure clear understanding between themselves and the group subsidiaries which use them.

It starts badly in that I'm immediately drawn into some complex issues on foreign exchange, particularly in the context of month-ends. Forex has never been a strong suit of mine, but fortunately the problem arises from the system of processing the information rather than the forex issues themselves, and the staff rectify it. Even so, it's a scary start; you always want to kick off a new project by scoring a quick goal, not by encountering something of which you have little knowledge.

An IT director once asked me "Why is it that whenever somebody hands you a problem, you start a spreadsheet?"

I hadn't been aware of the habit, but once he'd mentioned it I realised that it was my normal modus operandi. "Because," I answered (having had to think about it) "every problem has a set of independent variables and a set of dependent variables, and if you set them out in a grid you can actually see the shape of the problem, which often points you towards the solution. You learn much more by seeing than you do from listening. But if you hadn't asked, I wouldn't have realised that; I just did it instinctively."

Yes... people learn more by sight than by all the other senses, and setting a problem out in a grid format makes it much easier to understand than listening to someone describing it. The normal layout is to have the independent variables on one axis, with the dependent variables on the other.

We'd done the entire Sarbanes-Oxley project (number 29) on spreadsheets and it wouldn't have occurred to me to do it any other way. You could chart the various procedures against who were responsible, when the procedures should be done (immediately, weekly, etc.) and various other dependent factors. But I'd never rationalised it to myself until someone challenged me.

So to document the responsibilities of this group on my current project, I start a large but simple spreadsheet for each of the four main functions of the shared service centre: receivables, payables, cash and fixed assets (payroll is not included in the remit). Down the left side is a list of every possible procedure in the normal sequence of events (including some procedures not used; they are marked blank to show that they have been considered and not used, but can be activated if ever needed). There is a column for each company using the centre, including the centre itself, and a few columns for other purposes.

Simple codes are used for further detail in the cells themselves. The classic I, D, W, M, Q, Y for immediately, daily, weekly, monthly, quarterly, yearly, etc., is well-known and there are a few other abbreviations peculiar to the group.

That's the easy bit. But as in any organisation, you often get two different answers if you ask two people the same question. For good reasons, this organisation is no different; some subsidiaries have unique processing requirements and the spreadsheets begin to acquire a whole range of complexities, mostly dealt with by using letters or symbols in the boxes of the spreadsheet.

Occasionally we find that the client company and a member of the shared service centre give different answers to the same question and some resolution is needed. Each party has a different view of what happens, and in some cases what should happen. But for the most part, the subsidiaries and the centre are on identical lines, and the operation is smooth.

Another area to be looked at is the contracts between the subsidiaries and the centre itself. Firstly, all the contracts state that they are under UK law, a law which does not exist in the case of contracts. Scotland and Northern Ireland have different contract laws, and only England and Wales have the same law.

Moreover, the contracts list the responsibilities for the subsidiaries and the service centre, so that every time a procedure is changed (quite a frequent occurrence) the contract becomes progressively further out of date. The contract should simply make a generic reference to "procedures regularly updated and agreed between the parties". In that way, once a process change is agreed, it automatically becomes part of the contract without having to change the contract itself.

I raise the issue of the inappropriate contract formats with the group management, but they are uninterested, having much bigger issues to think about. Anyway, it is most unlikely that one part of the group will sue another part because of some failure to complete an internal contractual obligation!

With a lot of very specific assistance from the centre's managers and staff, the schedules are completed and agreed, and are later passed as acceptable by the external auditors. The one remaining problem is to ensure that there is a régime for ensuring that all changes are promptly and faithfully recorded and checked; but having recommended a procedure for doing that, I can only hope that they follow it rigorously after my departure. I think they do.

LESSONS

A. *In any situation involving the presentation of a high level of detail, and especially correlation between two major elements (usually* *dependent and independent), a matrix will be easier to construct, maintain and understand than a narrative format. The human mind learns 80% by sight and also retains visual images better than narratives.*

B. *Creating something is a satisfying process. Maintaining it is much harder, and usually gives much less satisfaction. The matrices will need maintenance!*

40. DIRECTOR DEVELOPMENT

Another job in Scotland... and a good one on which to finish. An adventurous and successful contracting company in the greater Glasgow area wishes to develop its financial controller to financial director level and I am given the task of coaching him. Fortunately he is ideal material, being equally happy with macro and micro issues, having an eagle eye for anything out-of-the-ordinary and also having a cheerful, straightforward personality.

We identify the following areas on which to work:

- a strong overview of the company as a whole
- knowledge of and confidence in the figures, and their implications for the ongoing performance of the company (no work is needed on the knowledge, as it happens, but considerable scope exists for improvement on the presentation of the figures)
- understanding of his co-directors and how he can support them
- knowledge of company law, particularly in relation to financial and structural matters
- personal influence at board and senior staff level
- control and development of subordinates in finance and administration (the financial director nearly always gets to look after the admin functions)

To give me an idea of the shape and size of the company, the first thing to do is to look at the most recent set of numbers, and here is the first shock (a double shock). The accounting is done on QuickBooks software, which was the software I encountered on the San Diego/ Los Angeles jaunt. No, no, no; you can't use that, I think in horror; it's ridiculously basic.

But the software has advanced hugely since then and is in fact ideal for this particular company, which runs contracts and therefore has numerous sub-ledgers. The more I see of the output from QuickBooks, the more I like it, and the more I like my protégé, whom I shall call Rory. He will probably teach me more than I teach him.

We agree a set of specific objectives based on the work areas listed above, and get going. It is a month-end, which is a bad time to start unless I shut up and watch and listen, which then turns it into a good time. Rory has a high work-rate, a good eye for details and anomalies and from his comments and curses it is clear that he also has a deep knowledge of the company's business, its customers and suppliers. This project is going to be fun.

All accounting software packages claim to produce an excellent suite of reports, but they rarely do, so I take an Excel reporting package I have built for a previous client and adapt it to this company's structure. In fact, the output end needs very little changing, but the input from the system of this company is colossal. Several hundred accounts codes are in use, so we create our own short suite of codes for reporting purposes and enter them opposite the 400-odd rows of output from the ledger. The SUMIF formula picks up this vast detail and totals it into the correct rows in the output reports.

We create a separate codes column for the output to give a manageable level of detail for the board papers and surround the sheet of inputs and outputs with check-totals. It is not unknown for errors to show up on one range as positive and another as negative, thereby cancelling out as zero in the error total.

The formula to avoid this is =MAX(range,0)-MIN(range,0). For example, an error of -21 and +21 in the same range will show as an error of 42 in the total error cell; they will not cancel out. A grand check-total of 0, summarising all the other check-totals is a very powerful and reassuring tool when hurriedly preparing version 7 of the results for the imminent board meeting!

A frequent (almost universal) criticism of company management is the lack of use of non-financial numbers. Once you start measuring your results against non-monetary figures such as quantities made and sold, sales areas, number of employees, hours worked, failure rates, miles travelled et cetera, the figures become considerably more meaningful. We have a lot of fun drawing up genuine statistics which will inform the board and target their thoughts precisely on the real issues.

Rory is a consummate raconteur and delights in surprising the board with quantified facts and trends of which they were unaware. By hitting on and emphasising different trends each month one can prevent board meetings from becoming stale. Business should never be "as usual"; if it is, it will soon atrophy.

The difficult part is in developing Rory's knowledge of company law. In the UK, "The Director's Handbook" edited by Martin Webster and published by Pinsent Masons provides the necessary knowledge in clear, well-summarised text, but it's up to Rory to do the reading. It's turgid stuff, but the book does a good job of making it readable and assimilable.

He applies himself well, and we have a weekly review of what he has learnt, and he retains the knowledge rather better than I do. Learning by rote is seldom an easy process. What really matters is that you can spot where a legal issue is likely to occur, and you know where to look to verify the situation.

He is doing well when there is a considerable upheaval caused by a merger of the company with a similar outfit in mainland Europe. A period of uncertainty regarding the board structure inevitably follows, but is eventually resolved. The managing director agrees that Rory is now well capable of operating at financial director level and that during (and probably after) the amalgamation with the European company I will be superfluous to requirements.

There are further developments, but they are not for this book.

LESSONS

A. *There is no one-size-fits-all learning plan for would-be directors, simply because every candidate has a different combination of knowledge and experience, and every company requires a different set of skills. However, the basic knowledge is compulsory for any financial director.*

B. *There are also a number of "soft" psychological skills which a director needs, but these vary with every occasion according to the director himself and to his colleagues and superiors, and to the needs and circumstances of the company. Moreover, one's fellow directors can be very different people from one issue to another, when sensitivities and concerns come to the fore.*

C. *Common sense is nevertheless the highest priority of all, especially in the way it needs to be applied differently according to each situation.*

EPILOGUE

At last I can retire... a strange sensation, but you get used to it. Eventually.

My overall reactions on having trawled through the previous 20 years and 40 projects are:

1. I have been extraordinarily lucky.

2. Most of that luck has come from the people with whom I've worked.

3. The rest of the luck was partly self-made, but more often fortuitous.

4. My wife has done an enormous amount of work to which it would have been reasonable to expect her husband to have contributed, if he hadn't been hundreds or even thousands of miles away, or at home claiming that he was too exhausted from the previous project to be able to do anything (funny, though, how he suddenly had loads of energy available when another project appeared). In addition to taming, developing and maintaining a large area of difficult and varied domestic hill ground, she also has business issues to control in addition to several other activities, and she dwarfs my meagre work output. I am more indebted to her than words can describe.

5. Some of the episodes in this book may be of encouragement or even practical use to others already in the interim director field, or considering going into that field, but do treat them warily. Although some projects quite closely resemble other projects, each one has enough characteristics of its own to ensure that you will encounter a new set of surprises and difficulties.

6. But if you, the reader, wish to spend some of your life in an interim director role, I wish you every success. Most importantly, do remember to enjoy it as you go. You will have many experiences that the average professional doesn't encounter, and most of those experiences will be positive. It's a very varied world out there, and you should sample as much of it as you can.

PART 3

THE 10 COMMANDMENTS

THE 10 COMMANDMENTS FOR INTERIM DIRECTORS

I confess that I didn't always obey these commandments in the early days, partly because they didn't exist in this form, and partly because I had no-one from whom to learn. However, things would undoubtedly have gone more smoothly if I had obeyed them!

1. GET SOME EXPERIENCE FIRST

This is the main commandment, and yet it was one that I didn't (and couldn't) obey. I did interim work because I had to, and it was pure luck that my first project turned out to be for a group that had every conceivable horror in its processes and a managing director who knew exactly how to fix many of the problems. His leadership rubbed off on his managers to the extent that we ourselves began to come up with clever, workable ideas to improve performance. We each began by knowing our own field, but by the time the businesses had been brought into profitability we were becoming capable all-rounders.

I also managed, more by luck than anything else, to recruit a very sparky and capable finance team, who taught me much more than I taught them.

However, if I'd gone into a business with a less able managing director and a less street-wise team, I would have struggled to do a job that just met the requirements and no more, and it might not have given me a suitable base of experience for whatever came next.

You should think of an interim job as an 80-20. You need to have 80% of the required experience at the outset, and the 20% which you pick up as you go along is a bonus, and also a step-up to being able to handle something more demanding in the future. Just as importantly, the 20% that you don't know keeps you on your toes and on the lookout for unforeseen traps and diversions.

Curiously, though, having 100% of the required experience and know-how can be dangerous. On the very few occasions when I've been (theoretically) 100% capable for a project it has taken the edge off my performance and I've been in danger of being slack. It would be wonderful if your projects were lined up in order of difficulty, but of course it doesn't work that way; a very tough number can be followed by a straightforward project, and you may tend to perform less sharply on the latter.

The adrenaline factor on a more difficult project is your friend; it keeps you sharp.

2. DON'T GO IN OVER YOUR HEAD

Many long-term interims have done this at one time or another. There's not much on the horizon and when an opportunity does turn up, you think "Well, it's not exactly me, but I can do that if I swot up a bit on [whatever] and learn it as I go along. I'll be able to get advice from [whomever] and it isn't exactly rocket science, is it?" Project 24 was a classic example.

Dangerous... even when you undertake a project for which your experience is suitable, there will be elements of that project which are difficult, or even entirely new to you. If the project itself is in an entirely new field, you will need a large slice of luck to come through unscathed.

However, you may encounter a situation where there is a shortage of suitable personnel and you are the nearest fit to the client's requirements. In such a situation, write an acceptance letter to the client stipulating that your experience does not cover certain specific areas and that the project will proceed on the basis that the client will provide that experience and input. I have had valuable assistance from client staff on very many occasions, and occasionally from another outsider working in parallel to her or his specific areas of knowledge and ability.

3. VERIFY THE REAL OBJECTIVES

On a number of occasions I had a project that turned out to be quite different from what I was told at the interview.

I've encountered three reasons for that:

- the client genuinely does not appreciate the full extent of the circumstances, in which case you should advise him of that at the interview and in your written acceptance, or if it does not become apparent until you are working on the project, report it immediately to your client, preferably in writing, together with a suggestion for remedy or improvement of the circumstances (for example, you may need additional skills to be available);
- during the project fresh internal developments occur which were not in force at commencement of the project, and which either complicate or change the direction of the project, in which case you should call a meeting to discuss how these developments will affect the business overall and your project specifically, and agree the appropriate action to be taken, confirming as above in writing;
- an external event occurs or changes materially the parameters of your work (or even prevents you from completing it as contracted), in which case you should notify your client immediately, and agree a revised course of action if necessary.

You may even find that a major internal or external change prevents you entirely from carrying out your agreed work. Again, this should ideally be notified to your client in writing. I had direct experience of that in project number 25, in which I had to fire the company which were to have provided my client with a worldwide payroll software package. In that particular case I presented it to my client as a fait accompli, as there simply wasn't time to spend arguing about it; I had to press ahead immediately to provide an alternative process before the group's overall accounting system deadline.

4. SMILE
A smile is an attitude, not a rictus.

You start the project as an unknown quantity, and it is important to get your client's staff onside with you very rapidly. Given that every person is different and that each person thinks and behaves differently in different circumstances, you will need to do a lot of listening, and if people are not forthcoming, you need to bring them out of their shells in a constructive way. To do this, you need an attitude which is positive and encouraging, and a smile is a major component of this approach.

One of the best ways to get people onside with you rapidly is to ask their advice. The fact that you consider someone to be knowledgeable and sensible enough to give you such advice is a subliminal statement that you respect their judgement. But be sure to ask advice that they are competent to give, so that they are pleased to have been consulted and can feel that they have made a worthwhile contribution. The most grumpy and unreasonable boss I ever had would always loosen up if I asked his advice, and consequently I phrased most of my conversations with him as requests for his opinion, my real requirement being hidden in the body of the ensuing conversation. I don't think he ever rumbled me.

Finally, whomever you have had a discussion with, you should thank them with a smile, and a confirmation that they have helped you. And if somebody is particularly helpful to you, don't forget to tell her/ his superior.

5. IDENTIFY STRONGLY WITH YOUR CLIENT
Don't use the word "you".

From the moment you start being interviewed for a project you should use the word "we" or "us", which aligns you one hundred per cent with your client. It says (not loud and clear, but subliminally) that you are an integral part of the client's business, even if it is only for a specific purpose and a specific period.

"If we can get a list of the tonnages and average prices, we can... ." is a typical "we" statement, neatly by-passing the dreaded "I".

However, don't overdo the old-pals act immediately on meeting a client, as it may appear presumptuous and eventually become annoying to the client. A reasonable sprinkling of the word "we" here and there will do just fine.

6. SCORE A QUICK GOAL

This should be a matter-of-fact action, and does not need to bear any relation to the project. From the moment you start the project you will be in observing and learning mode, and there is hardly a business on the planet that does not have some process or facility (or lack of one) that cannot be improved or remedied quickly without any song-and-dance.

During the interview for the project you may have identified something that your client needs to change or acquire and if you deal with that in your first day or two, it creates a remarkably good impression. Make sure that your client notices what you have done, but keep it low-key; a casual mentioning in passing will suffice.

They will thus regard you as "on-the-team" already.

7. WORK THROUGH YOUR CLIENT'S STAFF

When introducing new tasks or methods, get your client's staff to do as much as practicable of the work, so that after you have left, the expertise remains with the client. It may seem clever to have things become more difficult for your client after you've left, so that they miss you, but that situation will soon turn into annoyance that you haven't done the job fully.

This may occur even if the final piece of work isn't part of your remit. If you see that the business is not going to obtain the full benefit of your work because of some inadequacy elsewhere, you must make sure that that inadequacy is rectified during your time with the client. If this cannot be done, you should report to the client in writing the restriction on the effectiveness and preferably define what should be done to overcome the problem.

The more you work alone, the more you will be held responsible (often wrongly) for situations over which you have no control. Therefore ensure that your client does his share of the work, and also that he is kept up to date at all times with progress and problems (present and forthcoming). And as I have stated before, asking client staff for their advice is a good way of keeping them "on the team" and au fait with what is happening.

8. GET HELP, ESPECIALLY AT THE START

There are two kinds of help you will need:

- getting established in the first place
- dealing with whatever requirements or obstacles rear their heads during the project

Both of these require forethought.

As soon as you have had an adequate briefing on the project, you should provide a list of requirements, ranging from office space and facilities to travel and access documents, accommodation, technical support, access to the necessary personnel and systems, and other arrangements.

Your client's administrators will need your passport details and possibly the passport itself for visas and travel tickets and you should be ready to deal with these straight after the interview. In some cases, if you are the successful candidate, the client wants you to get going immediately, and it doesn't look clever to have to drive 200 miles home and back to get your passport and some clothes. Your first two main allies are usually the boss's secretary and the IT department, and they will rapidly point you towards the other players you need.

Nobody seems to check much on inoculations these days, but do consider them and keep them up-to-date. If you are being interviewed for a job overseas, you should be able to say that your passport and inoculations are in date. In a case of great emergency that may even get you the assignment instead of another applicant who will have to wait to get his paperwork completed.

Be aware that some countries black-list other countries, and if your passport shows that you have been in a black-listed country, your application to go to the country which your client needs you to visit may be refused. If you work internationally, keep up to date with the pressure points, so that you can anticipate and avoid any difficulties. I held three passports at one time!

I was once booked on a flight from Nashville to Mexico City (S-Ox business) when a big phlegmatic African-American checked my passport prior to my entering the departure lounge. He looked at my passport slowly, page-by-page, a frown deepening on his face, and my heart sank. Stamped in the passport were some of the favourite enemies of Uncle Sam, and I had visions of a long Toronto-style interview with an official of the CIA. But after a minute or so the official's frown turned into a slow smile and he handed me back my passport, saying "Man, you are one well-travelled dude." I thanked him and resumed my normal respiratory cycle.

A European and an Asia Pacific phrase-book are handy items for your brief- case, for obvious reasons. In the case of an interview for a project in a foreign country, establish from the outset what is needed to operate there in terms of documents, health, currency, language, transport, accommodation and other forms of local support. Also, learn the local politeness and rudeness, especially in Asia Pacific. Certain actions and gestures common in the West are considered offensive (or at least uncouth) in the East.

Lonely Planet, Colllins and Berlitz publish excellent pocket guides for foreign countries, and in many cases can provide CDs for the related languages. And beware: people in other countries do not always speak with the same accents that you hear in the movies! That applies especially to Eastern European nations, who certainly don't sound as if they're in a cold-war spy flick.

You will often need the client's IT department to set you up on their systems, both at your main base and at any other client sites you need to visit. The laptop with which they provide you will have to operate in the countries you will be visiting. Some interims work with their own laptops, but that makes them responsible for any problems that occur with them, and in any event, some clients will not let you link in an external computer to their network.

9. DON'T OPERATE IN ISOLATION

Establish your prime contacts within your client's organisation from the outset (even before you start, preferably). The boss's secretary is numero uno.

Prepare beforehand a list of what you will need from each of them, so that they can have everything ready for you when you start. There are few things more infuriating than arriving at a client's premises and being unable to start work. The client doesn't like it either!

Interim projects vary enormously from one to another unless you are a specialist in a particular field or industry, but your list of admin requirements will nevertheless be fairly consistent from one role to another. Technical requirements, however, will naturally vary from one project to the rest, and you should identify and request these at your interview if it is politic (and why shouldn't it be?).

The more you operate with the client's technology and staff, the more you will be identified as being committed to their objectives.

10. LEAVE YOUR EXPERTISE BEHIND WITH THE CLIENT

It may seem clever to ride off into the sunset at the end of the project with all of the knowledge in your head and your files, but that is not the behaviour of a professional.

Make sure that when you finish your project(s) your client has all the tools and skills needed to continue successfully from where you have finished. In most interim projects, you should ideally be doing some tutoring, or at least advising, throughout your time with your client. And make sure that your tutoring covers all the relevant staff levels, from the tea-boy to the chairman.

You may think that this would deprive you of some further work, but the reverse is true. The more projects you do well, the more your former clients will want you back, and the more likely they are to recommend you to other potential clients.

And remember, when advising client staff you should be careful not to talk down to them. A useful way of giving advice without appearing to lecture someone is to relate the advice via a mythical third party, with a line such as "I once saw someone do [something clever]". In that way, you can pass on the method you are trying to instil in the client without appearing to give advice.

Finally, ensure that your clients can contact you after you have left, in case they have any subsequent queries. It would be a grave mistake to spoil a well-conducted project for the sake of one or two small queries... they may even be looking for you to do more work for them! If I do not hear from a client, I give them a call back after an appropriate length of time to ensure that they are not having difficulty with any aspect of my project work.

A happy client makes for a happy interim director.

Good luck!

PART 4

HOW TO GET WORK AS AN
INTERIM DIRECTOR

Your personality

There is no hard-and-fast rule on personality. Extroverts, introverts, inbetweenoverts and all manner of characters are out there in the field, operating successfully and happily. However, there are some basic functional requirements, regardless of character:

- you must be able to get along happily and constructively with the people above, below and alongside you in your projects, and especially with customers of your client (if the people with whom you work are not happy, it's harder for them to be constructive, even when they're trying to)

- although you should make every effort to work in harmony with your client staff, there may be occasions when you have to put your foot down or go out on a limb on an issue, and if you are certain you are right you will have to explain your actions as firmly and constructively as practicable; clarity of expression is therefore an important attribute

- you may even have to eat humble pie in respect of occurrences which are no fault of yours (sometimes you have only a second or two to decide whether to argue strongly or concede a point that you consider to be incorrect, inappropriate or even unjust)

- you must be honest; I've usually found it much easier to admit a mistake than to try and hide it, and in some cases that has even raised my stock with the client, who realises that he will get the truth instead of some convoluted excuse (but don't make mistakes too often!)

- you need to keep the client informed of progress; it's better to be telling him what is happening than for him to be searching all over the building (or sometimes all over the planet) trying to find out what stage you have reached and whether things are going satisfactorily . . . secretive people do not usually make good interims

- you should also keep the client informed of non-minor problems (preferably in advance, in most cases), the bad news always being less unacceptable coming from you than from somebody else

- don't be afraid to ask the client for advice; as long as you're not asking a stupid question (but we all do that occasionally) it usually conveys to the client that you're concerned to get things exactly in line with the client's requirements

- and when the project or a major element thereof is completed, put in a short written report to the client summarising the work done, just to remind the client of the value he is getting from your fee (in your weekly invoices you should put a reasonable amount of detail, to remind the client that he is benefitting from your work and that the benefit is worth the fee)

In conclusion, do as you would be done by; that applies to almost any job, but as an interim you have a very short time in which to make a positive impact, so your personality must be positive from the moment you begin the project.

Your experience

General – be it technical, commercial, managerial, directorial, political, scientific or whatever, you must have 80-90% of the experience appropriate and specific to the role or the project.

That doesn't mean that you must have done the identical work before, but you need to have successfully performed similar and relevant work. And don't worry about the minor bits that you haven't done before; they will keep you on your toes and prevent you from getting sloppy.

If you're a specialist in a certain type of work, it will be easier for you to gain momentum in a project, since you are already playing to your strengths. Generalists have to work harder in adapting to many of the roles they undertake, so do notify your client at an early stage of any technical or other assistance you may need from the client's staff (or possibly their advisors).

The fear factor? It's natural to be apprehensive when starting a project, but that keeps you on your toes. Note down all your queries and concerns and resolve them with the client at an early stage. If you do that sensibly, the client will recognise that you are being both organised and thorough. However, once you work up a head of steam, your queries should be bigger and fewer.

Your CV

The main purpose of a CV is to differentiate you positively from all of the other candidates vying for your intended project. It's what gets you the interview, and the interview is what gets you the project . . . if you handle the interview well.

So laying your CV out in a strictly conventional format with all the usual clichés ("I am an energetic, committed, goal-oriented . . ." etc) is not going to distinguish you from the rest of the pack.

On the other hand, a CV which is so unconventional as to be bizarre won't help you either with most clients. The content must be relevant and sensible, with appropriate wording and/or layout which distinguishes you from other applicants. English is one of the richest languages in the world, so if your CV is in English, there is no excuse for failing to come up with wording which is distinctive but still relevant and appropriate.

I presented my CV in landscape rather than portrait layout, which meant that almost everyone who received it remembered it (even if they didn't like it, they would contact me if there was relevant work afoot). With one exception, I refused to use a conventional portrait format.

The first 30% of width of the CV gave my personal details, contact address et cetera, and the other 70% covered my career.

In bold print in the career section I listed in bullet-points all of the types of work I had done, in purely generic terms. Even if your work has been fairly conventional, if you think back carefully you can list a number of different activities and experiences which will be relevant to your clients and their projects.

Putting these in bold bullet-points makes them stand out from the general narrative and zeros the potential client (or the recruiter choosing candidates) in on your main attributes. It also makes your CV stand out from other CVs. However, restrict the use of bold print to section headings and the list of your capabilities.

Don't waste any space describing how you are a highly-motivated, self-starting, results-focused, objective-driven pragmatic leader/team-player, or whatever other clichés come to mind. The more of these nonsensical terms there are on your CV, the less likely anyone is to believe them. It's what you've done and can do that matter on your CV, and the personal characteristics can be demonstrated by giving sensible answers at the interview.

Many recruitment agencies insist in a house style, so that all of the CVs they hold look the same. They do this so that they can access their databases to extract rapidly a selection of candidates to meet a client's requirement.

From the point of view of the client, who is usually seeking someone of calibre, this is not helpful. On occasions when I have been recruiting on behalf of a client, I have always insisted on being given the candidates' own CVs in the format in which they were designed. This has resulted in documents ranging from one sheet to five sheets, for the same post, and tells me much more about the candidates than a house style does.

Finally, always consider whether your CV is exactly right for the interim post for which you are applying; you may need to tweak it to suit as closely as possible the client's requirements as advertised (as far as you can ascertain those). Previous work which is especially relevant to the project for which you are applying may need to be especially prominent on your CV.

You will have noticed that the above points refer similarly to applications for permanent posts and for consultancy or other technical projects. What the client is looking for is much the same: capability and compatibility. Having been a director of Company X is useful experience on your CV, but having managed some major projects or developments is much more useful. It's not where you've been that counts; it's what you've done.

Employment agencies

Employment agencies have been good to me. My main sources have been in the UK, in Edinburgh, Newcastle-upon-Tyne and especially along the M62, and these areas have provided about 60-70% of my work (including overseas assignments) in terms of time worked. The M62 corridor has a vibrant and direct work culture, only equalled in Britain by Glasgow.

Capital cities present a more difficult prospect for the project hunter, because of the sheer extent and density of population, and also their perception of themselves. Such cities tend to think that anyone from beyond their travel-to-work area is of a lower calibre. I shall refrain from commenting further on that attitude!

The remaining 30-40% of my work has come from my own contacts, who have materialised more by accident than by my efforts. Although I've ridden my luck rather than obtain work by cold-calling, there is now much more competition out there, and I recommend to prospective interims that you make a specific effort to build up a network of recruitment agencies who handle interim work. There is at least one major UK recruitment company which specialises heavily in interim assignments, and this company and many others are well established and highly effective.

However, you may find it worthwhile getting yourself on the candidate lists of agencies who deal specifically in permanent posts, as some of their clients will have interim requirements and the agencies will be reluctant to allow this work to go to their competitors. Nevertheless, I have encountered agencies who steadfastly refuse to handle interim work (until it crops up very advantageously and makes them think again).

Overseas assignments are harder to obtain than ones in your own territory. The most common route to finding work in Europe is through European subsidiaries of UK (and occasionally US) companies.

You may find recruitment firms who do not handle interim assignments. Just leave your CV with them and move on! When one of their most important clients wants an interim, they will respond quickly lest they lose their client's mainstream business, and eventually they will realise the value of interims.

Other routes

Going freelance with your existing employer is often a good starting point. Typically, an employer no longer has full-time work for one of its staff, and that person goes freelance with a dedicated percentage or number of hours working as a contractor to the erstwhile employer.

The ex-employee then approaches other companies (directly or through an agency) and builds up a portfolio of occasional clients. One of two things usually happens here: either the ex-employee builds up a network of clients to create a manageable portfolio of work, or s/he survives financially on the single client until s/he can find another permanent role.

Most people who have moved around professionally keep in touch with previous colleagues and employers. Putting out diplomatic feelers for project work with people who already know your capabilities may yield opportunities. And there is no harm in putting out a flier with your CV to potential targets in your area; it costs little and may yield a result.

Chats and lunches (at your expense!) to catch up with previous contacts from whom you've drifted apart can be rewarding. They may have opportunities, and they may also know of other businesses who are looking for assistance. But people will gradually forget you if you don't keep in touch.

Networking . . . never miss an opportunity to tell business people or their contacts that you are operating as an interim. And if times are tough, don't tell anybody except your closest confidants (and only those who can be trusted to keep that in confidence). As far as the outside world is concerned, things are going swimmingly.

The reason for this is a strange but well-known dynamic which is a corollary of Murphy's Law: if you are busy, lots of people want you, but if you're not busy, nobody wants to know. So don't say you can meet someone any day; tell them you're busy on days X and Y, but can manage days W or Z, depending on the time. So remember: to the outside world you are almost NEVER unemployed.

In smaller towns, it may be worth contacting local firms of accountants to advise them of your experience and availability. However, I have no direct or indirect experience of that.

IIM (Institute for Interim Management)

The IIM are an organisation specifically established to develop, support and advise the interim director profession, and it would be well worth your while contacting them. Their website is at http://iim. org.uk/ and is a gold-mine of information and advice for both new and experienced interim directors.

Take the time to study their website in detail, and once you have done that you will be much better placed to decide how to proceed. The early days in an interim director's career can be lonely at times, and it's reassuring to have some friendly professional back-up on your side.

Interview technique

If you play the whole interview dead straight you risk boring the interviewer. If on the other hand you overdo the joking, you will become irritating. The middle course is what you should be seeking, but sprinkled with occasional touches of humour and individuality to demonstrate a suitable personality.

SMILE. They are looking for someone positive! However, they may also be looking for sensitivity, so use the right kind of smile:

- the positive smile, which says "Yes, I can do that"
- the sympathetic smile, which shows understanding
- the humorous smile, which shows you're human and easy to get along with
- the hard smile, which shows that you appreciate the toughness of the situation being discussed

However, you should remain serious for the great majority of the time. The interview for an interim post will be a different proposition from one for a permanent post, because:

- they need you to hit the ground running; you are very unlikely to have the kind of lead-in time allowed for a permanent post
- you will have a shorter time to gel with your new colleagues than you would have for a permanent role, so your personality will be of great importance to the interviewer

- in many cases you will be much more exposed in both culture and working style; collaborating and arguing with a Birmingham office when you're in Sydney is very different from doing it face-to-face, where your facial expressions and body language are important assets if you use them sensitively
- in most interim assignments the skills required will tend towards project management rather than strategic management, so you need to be able to convince the client that you can adapt to the different parameters, especially the constraints, and grasp the priorities of the project firmly and rapidly.

Home life

The peripatetic life was relatively easy for me; I have no offspring and a highly independent wife who handles a heavy and varied workload effectively and without assistance. She was also able to join me for short periods in various countries. But the majority of people at interim director level have a wide range of domestic responsibilities which cannot easily be put aside.

You have three choices:

- only accept projects in your home area (that must therefore be a highly urban area, to generate enough projects)
- adapt yourself and your family to long periods apart
- take your partner with you on projects (not likely to be a suitable arrangement for either of you in the longer term, but usually most enjoyable for short periods).

Getting on the ladder

Unless you have a major slice of luck, you will have to do quite a bit of work both to get started and to gain momentum. To start with, as stated above, you must create a CV that specifically identifies you as a suitable candidate for the type of work at which you are aiming (see earlier section).

Then you need to visit a range of recruitment agencies which cover the areas (geographic and technical) in which you intend to work. Some of them have specialist interim recruiters, who are the people to target first.

Second in line are the recruiters who look after large companies, who tend to have more staff changes than smaller businesses, and therefore more temporary opportunities. A point here is that large companies are usually easier to work for, as they tend to have clearly defined roles to be filled, whereas projects with smaller companies tend to start out simply and rapidly branch out into a variety of concurrent objectives. Small companies are therefore usually more fun to work for, but you often need a wider range of experience to meet their needs.

By the way, I use the word "fun" deliberately. Even in the toughest of jobs, there should be laughter, and an occasional piece of relevant light-heartedness in interviews with recruiters will not go amiss. The projects in which I have gained momentum most rapidly are those in which the client staff have a well-developed sense of humour.

Press adverts are not often used for temporary positions, but you should check a selection of appropriate newspapers readily.

While this is happening, make a list of all of the companies with which you have had dealings in your previous business life and where you have suitable contacts. Customers, suppliers, lawyers, auditors . . . any of them may be aware of a situation needing handling for a period. Let each company know that you are available for projects by contacting them individually with an approach tailored to the specific relationship which you have had with them. One size does not fit all. But beware of breaching any restrictions which may have been imposed upon you in respect of the termination of your previous employment.

Where you have had a specific positive connexion with any individual in these familiar companies, a more personal approach would be advisable. A sociable lunch in which you mention your availability without pushing too strongly may well sow a few seeds in the mind of a contact who has various issues needing handled.

One very important point: you are always busy!

It is a strange but undeniable corollary of Murphy's Law that people are more likely to want you when you are doing something else, and less likely to want you when you are available. Therefore, even if you're just helping a friend clear out his garage, as far as the outside world is concerned you're on a stock reduction project. But don't overdo the hyperbole.

Summary

You must be able to do most or all of these:

- have accumulated sufficient depth and breadth of capability in your chosen field(s)
- operate at the appropriate level of responsibility
- be an effective team director and manager (even if you have a solo role, you are likely to have to influence external people, sometimes against their perception)
- be able to operate in an unfamiliar or even alien environment
- be able to get team members, and sometimes your superiors, onside with your objectives (ie the individual objectives necessary to meet the client's overall objective) and mode of operation
- be able to commandeer the resources needed for the project
- be capable in three different modes: ongoing situations, project environments and management of controlled change
- (occasionally and carefully) be able to make decisions against the perceived direction or ethos of your client
- be able to justify those decisions!

The above list of requirements may appear daunting, but when you think about them you will realise that you need to meet similar requirements from time to time in your regular work.

GO FOR IT!

BY THE SAME AUTHOR
"THE FINANCIAL CONTROLLER"

The Financial Controller is a field encyclopaedia of some 400 pages, written for all finance professionals, both in industry and in advisory capacities. It covers every aspect of running a tough, happy and successful business, and has become recognised as the essential bible for the finance professional in industry, and for those who advise industry professionals.

Unusually for a financial text, it deals extensively with the subject of the people in a business, and their duties, concerns, personal development, problems and organisational structures. It also contains a large number of real-life business examples, ranging from the ridiculous to the ingenious.

The book contains the following major sections, all of them practical:

- The personnel section covers all levels of people from the chairman to the operatives, and highlights the objectives, responsibilities, duties and environments of all of the main players in the business. It also deals with all of the main external players relevant to the business and how these relationships can be most successfully developed and sustained.

- The numbers section covers the full range of accounting and control activities, from the shop floor numbers through to the figures presented to the outside world.

- The performance section concentrates on using the numbers to maximise the performance of the business.

- The systems section of 100 pages is a comprehensive guide to the financial systems and their structures for any manufacturing or trading business. It has been used as a successful Sarbanes-Oxley platform in 10 countries.

- The controls section covers a number of other protective issues, such as insurance, legal matters and fraud prevention.

- The appendices contain a large selection of formats of top-end management information, many of the formats being fundamentally different from traditional layouts and considerably more informative.

INDEX

(index references are to project numbers)